Faith Alone

THE WAY TO CHRIST

Spiritual Living in Light of God's Grace

Faith Alone
THE WAY TO CHRIST

Spiritual Living in Light of God's Grace

by

Matthew Correll

Wonderment
Simplicity
Grace
Love
Joy
✝

Faith Alone
THE WAY TO CHRIST
Spiritual Living in Light of God's Grace

Special Thanks to:

Arianna!

David Cray for evocative editing.

John Correll for printing and other editorial advice.

Gary Roberts for asking lots of questions.

And, of course: Jesus Christ, God the Father and the Holy Spirit!

Contents

Foreword

This book is another revelation of God's marvelous grace. I hope to provide more insight into the doctrine of free grace and in turn hope to encourage my readers to live out the free grace message in their daily lives. I'd like to start off by giving the gospel invitation in case my reader has never been saved.

The Gospel Invitation

God gives eternal life to anyone who wants it. It is free. It is a gift. But it is also our choice.

Deuteronomy 30:19 — *I call heaven and earth to record this day against you, that I have set before you life and death, blessing and cursing: therefore choose life, that both thou and thy seed may live.*

Anyone who goes to hell ... goes willingly.

Nobody goes to hell by mistake or chance, but by choice.

Titus 2:11 — *For the grace of God that bringeth salvation hath appeared to all men.*

Salvation is found in the scriptures. John 3:15-18.

All you have to do is believe that Jesus died for your sins and that by believing you will have eternal life.

Ephesians 2:1 — *And you hath he quickened, who were dead in trespasses and sins.*

Other passages say, "quickened together" which literally means to reanimate conjointly. The idea is to be brought into eternal life with God by spiritual rebirth. This happens by faith alone in the Lord Jesus Christ.

Let me continue by giving you a litany of Sola Fide quotes from the Bible.

Thy faith hath saved thee. Matthew 9:22.

Thy faith hath made thee whole. Matthew 5:34.

Believe only. Luke 8:50.

You are saved through faith. Ephesians 2:8.

Jesus saw their faith, thy sins be forgiven thee. Mark 2:5.

Have faith in God. Mark 11:22.

****

The following subsets are to explain this marvelous doctrine in greater detail, hence looking at it from several different angles. This book is to remind us of God's free grace. My desire is that this book will show us how to respond to grace in faithful, spiritual living. E.g., ... evangelism, Bible studies, making your own gospel tracts, etc. Too often, we are reminded of God's unceasing, illimitable grace without any motivational follow-up to live after the spirit

God bless!

Chapter 1

Mental Assent

M ost people in our churches today will deny that saving faith is simply bare mental assent of Christ's finished work. They try to make salvation difficult. Some say that you have to seek God with all your heart. Mental assent seems to be too easy. You have to have a deeper or more emotional faith in order to be saved. But is this correct? According to the Bible, No!

Such anti-mental-assenters will use the verse in James as their staple proof-text.

James 2:19 — *Thou believest that there is one God; thou doest well: the devils also believe, and tremble.*

They call this demonic faith. They try to qualify this faith with habitual sin or carnal living. Some will say something to the effect of: "He lives in sin. He doesn't have real, true 'saving faith." Even the demons believed but they were not saved."

The demons had epistemic knowledge of who Christ was but demons have no way to be saved. Their fate was and is sealed. Believing that there is one God is simply monotheism. Islam believes that Allah is the one true God. This doesn't mean that Moslems or demons have asked Christ to save them. Demons couldn't get saved even if they wanted to. (2 Peter 2:4.) James 2:19, is a frail straw man argument in opposing the doctrine of mental assent.

Romans 10:10 — *For with the heart man believeth unto right-eousness; and with the mouth confession is made unto salvation.*

The word heart in the Greek is: *Kardia.* Which means, "mind" or "intellect." With the mind man believeth unto righteousness, sounds like mental assent to me.

A preacher has said that believing in Christ for salvation is: quote, the act of assenting to something understood. But understanding alone is not belief in what is understood.

Unquote.

Why does mental assent save us? Because it excludes works of any kind. (Romans 4:16.) Mental assent works because of the object of our faith. The object is Christ and the object is precious. It is also the object that is sufficient. Mental assent is the simplest way man must procure this precious, eternal object—which is Christ! Now mental assent sounds absurd if the object is not on Christ. Mental assent in any other thing would be nonsensical. Mental assent in a carrot or a rock would be absurd. But a rock and a carrot cannot save anyone. Christ can and because He did all the work at Calvary, mental assent is enough. The way I put it is that if a person wants to be saved, then all he has to do is believe in Jesus, such a belief, which excludes works, has to be mental assent!

We need to focus on the object of what is saving us and not our faith or the degrees thereof.

Faith fluctuates and sometimes even fizzles out!

But the faithfulness of Christ can never fail.

Hebrews 10:23 — *Let us hold fast the profession of our faith without wavering; (for he is faithful that promised.)*

The author of Hebrews encourages his readers to hold fast to their profession of faith but even if they don't he explains that God is faithful. There's no better way to undergird such an encouragement, but to assure Christians that God will always be faithful no matter what.

Yes, we are saved by faith alone in Christ. The doctrine of mental assent is the only way I can proclaim this without being in err or resorting into some kind of paganized ritualistic faith. To say that mental assent is not what it means to believe in Christ for salvation is to render faith into a work—even if it is just the work of emotion.

Mental assent that Christ died for our sins makes salvation as easy as can be. Some may oppose this by saying that mental assent is not the same as trusting Christ personally for salvation and that may be true. We need to trust Christ in a personal and relational fashion, but to say that mental assent cannot confirm this is wrong.

If someone said that they met the president yesterday, wouldn't believing this be tantamount to mental assent? No one would question the degree or veracity of their faith.

The words, "mental assent" or "bare intellectual assent" shouldn't even be used in our theological literature.

Faith Alone. THE WAY TO CHRIST.

Chapter 2

The Metaphors of Faith

Faith in Christ is so simple that the Bible likens it to merely looking upon God. That's too easy some might be thinking. With such a notion of simplicity, some people might be getting saved inadvertently just by looking at a picture of Jesus hung high on a church wall. Or by watching the Passion Of The Christ and then thinking that on judgment day they will be justified because they visually saw Jim Caviezel playing the role of Jesus.

That's not what I'm talking about. Yes, looking to Christ is the same as coming to Him in faith, but a desire to be saved must take precedence.

God is not going to force anyone to be saved and He isn't going to save someone by accident either. Nobody will be in heaven because they were like a deer in headlights upon some bright; blinding epiphany and conversely, nobody will be in hell because they never heard the gospel.

Romans 1:20 — *For the invisible things of him from the creation of the world are clearly seen, being understood by the things that are made, even his eternal power and Godhead; so that they are without excuse.*

See also Psalms 19:1-4 and Colossians 1:23.

The Bible also says.

Revelation 22:17 — *And the Spirit and the bride say, Come. And let him that heareth say, Come. And let him that is athirst come. And whosoever will, let him take the water of life freely.*

This makes it clear that salvation is free for the taking and easy to obtain.

That's why it is important to get the correct gospel message out and about. This may sound like a contradiction, but it is not. Anyone who is honestly seeking will get the free grace message of the gospel because those proof-text verses are the simplest in the Bible to understand. "Free gift," "Not of works," He that believes," "whoever drinks will never thirst again," "shall never perish." It is Satan and man's supercilious pride that eclipse this biblical truth about free grace.

And quite frankly, most people who don't like free grace are too afraid to humble themselves and admit that they need a Saviour and furthermore that they are helplessly in their sins without Christ.

So back to what I was saying. Without a proper faith alone gospel, the true, selfless desire to be a Christian would be mislaid. The thing is however for those who want to be saved from hell; it is as easy as looking upon God at one moment of time.

Scripture reinforces this.

Isaiah 45:22 — *Look unto me, and be ye saved, all the ends of the earth: for I am God, and there is none else.*

The idea of looking to God denotes the punctiliarity of salvation by faith. "Punctiliar" simply means that it took place in a moment's time and still eternally continues forevermore. The reason the Bible compares simple faith with looking is to show us that it is not a drawn-out stare or a succession of serial looks, but just one, initial look that enters us into eternal salvation. There will be more on this verse, (45:22) in my subset entitled: Christ in Isaiah.

Even back in the Noahic times was the metaphor of looking used to signify the reception of salvation.

Genesis 9:16 — *And the bow* (rainbow) *shall be in the cloud; and I will <u>look</u> upon it, that I may remember the everlasting covenant between God and every living creature of all flesh that is upon the earth.*

Even the prophet Isaiah used such sensory language to describe the simplicity of salvation.

Isaiah 55:3 — *Incline your ear, and come unto me: hear, and your soul shall live; and I will make an everlasting covenant with you, even the sure mercies of David.*

John 5:25 — *Verily, verily, I say unto you, The hour is coming, and now is, when the dead shall hear the voice of the Son of God: and they that hear shall live.*

This is not saying that hearing about God is enough to be saved, for willful belief must follow. It is however illustrating that coming to God is as simple as just hearing Him.

In the book of Numbers, Moses used the same metaphor. When his followers were snakebitten, he gave them the simple instruction to look upon the fiery serpent.

Numbers 21:8 — *And the LORD said unto Moses, Make thee a fiery serpent, and set it upon a pole: and it shall come to pass, that every one that is bitten, when he looketh upon it, shall live.*

Most people say that God is good but they fail to understand why or how they believe it. So many people will deny that salvation can be possessed irrevocably in the blink of an eye. They will allude to the fact that man must do more than just have a moment's belief. Man must have to do something else, like persevere, repent of sin or do good works. In such a case, it wouldn't matter if God were good or not. It would only matter if man were being good. God's goodness would be supplanted by man's labors and pride.

This is why the free grace doctrine is failsafe. In fact, this is the only doctrine that doesn't malign God's character. It's the only doctrine that gives man absolutely no bragging rights.

Faith Alone. THE ONLY WAY TO CHRIST.

Chapter 3

The Just By Faith Shall Live

All attacks on free grace are fire-powered by sinful pride and backboned by twisting scripture out of context. Most people add biases to the meaning of scripture. For instance, let's say that someone is inclined to believe that salvation is about persisting in the faith. To them, such negligence to live on in the faith means that the person isn't saved at all. This is how a person can justify calling his fellow brother a false Christian—but is this biblical? The answer is, no!

Someone may take this verse and twist the meaning to fit their theological bias.

Romans 1:17 — *For therein is the righteousness of God revealed from faith to faith: as it is written, The just shall live by faith.*

They may say that the just (saved) will live by faith, in other words, remain in the faith in order to prove the legitimacy of their salvation. But is this really what this verse implies?

Read the latter part of the verse again. *The just shall live by faith.* Reading from the KJV may lead someone to the idea that because of someone's justification, they will live by faith in order to prove that they are saved. But it shouldn't be translated this way. It should be read as: the just shall live *because* of faith. In other words, if you are saved by faith you have eternal life. Other translations such as the NLT read differently. But for the sake of KJV-similarity, I've chosen the Young's Literal translation.

Romans 1:17 — *For the righteousness of God in it is revealed from faith to faith, according as it hath been written, 'And the righteous one by faith shall live.'*

Galatians 3:11, is also translated this way by the Young's literal Bible. *And that in law no one is declared righteous with God, is evident, because 'The righteous by faith shall live.'*

Nowhere does it say that one must live by faith after being saved in order to keep or prove their salvation. Nowhere. It simply reads that the just, (who are justified by faith) because of faith shall have eternal life. There is no guarantee that they will live a faithful life— not even ten seconds after being saved.

Operational Death

Romans 7, is an example of trying to obey the law by man's ability. Paul, as a Christian, explains that it just can't be done. But have you ever considered that the "Holy Spirit" is not mentioned in Romans 7. Romans 8, however, describes the activity of the Holy Spirit in our daily walk.

Take a look at the 8th chapter of Romans.

Let me explain what "death" means in these passages. Death refers to operational death, which means persistent carnal living, not physical death, spiritual death or any other kind of death. Before we exegetically take on Romans 8, let's take a look at the different types of death in the Bible.

There are 7 types of death described in the Bible.

Spiritual death. (Ephesians 2:1.)

Physical death. (Matthew 8:22.)

Sexual death. (Hebrews 11:11-12.)

Positional death. 2 Timothy 2:11.)

Eternal death. (Revelation 20:15.)

Carnal death. (Ephesians 5:14.)

Operational death. (Romans 8:6.)

****

Operational death is in view here.

C denotes: Christian. *NC* denotes: non-Christian.

1—*There is therefore now no condemnation to them which are in Christ Jesus, who walk not after the flesh, but after the Spirit.* *C*

If you are saved, then you are in Christ positionally. (1 John 5:20.) And there is no condemnation, not now, not ever—no matter what you do!

2—*For the law of the Spirit of life in Christ Jesus hath made me free from the law of sin and death.* *C*

"Law of sin" means penalty of sin. "Death" refers to operational death, which means living in invariable, long-term carnality.

3—*For what the law could not do, in that it was weak through the flesh, God sending his own Son in the likeness of sinful flesh, and for sin, condemned sin in the flesh.* *C*

This is referring to the Mosaic Law and it asserts that the law can neither justify a sinner nor give them spiritual regeneration.

4—*That the righteousness of the law might be fulfilled in us, who walk not after the flesh, but after the Spirit.* *C*

There are two types of Christian behavior. Walking in the flesh and walking in the spirit. (Ephesians 5:8.) Some theological systems don't agree that there can be a carnal Christian, but scripture supports in many places that some Christians are carnal. (1 Corinthians 3:1. Romans 7:14. 1 Thessalonians 5:10.)

5—*For they that are after the flesh do mind the things of the flesh; but they that are after the Spirit the things of the Spirit.*

This verse describes both types of sinners. "After" is the key word.

6—*For to be carnally minded is death; but to be spiritually minded is life and peace.*

Death once again refers to operational death. "Spiritually minded" doesn't mean sinless, it simply means that there is spiritual activity in the life of such believers. *C*

7—*Because the carnal mind is enmity against God: for it is not subject to the law of God, neither indeed can be.* *C* ...*NC*

Both Christians and non-Christians can be in enmity against God.

8—*So then they that are in the flesh cannot please God.* *NC*

"In the flesh" is antithetical to, "in Christ." Believers are <u>in</u> Christ positionally, but may walk <u>after</u> the flesh. This verse is exclusively referring to unbelievers for they cannot walk in the spirit at all yet the believer has a choice as to whether they walk in the spirit or in the flesh.

9—*But ye are not in the flesh, but in the Spirit, if so be that the Spirit of God dwell in you. Now if any man have not the Spirit of Christ, he is none of his.*

Believers are never characterized by being: "in the flesh" although they can and do walk "after the flesh" as scripture clearly illustrates.

Carnal believers may walk after the flesh but positionally they are still in Christ. (Romans 6:6.)

10—*And if Christ be in you, the body is dead because of sin; but the Spirit is life because of righteousness.*

11—*But if the Spirit of him that raised up Jesus from the dead dwell in you, he that raised up Christ from the dead shall also quicken your mortal bodies by his Spirit that dwelleth in you.*

12—*Therefore, brethren, we are debtors, not to the flesh, to live after the flesh.*

Notice the wording, "after the flesh." This is warning us not to live after the flesh. We are saved by grace and are positionally in Christ; so that is why we shouldn't live after the flesh. This is not talking about periodic sins, for all are guilty even the most spiritual Christians. (Ecclesiastes 7:20.) Living after the flesh is like a twenty-four/seven thing and we are warned not to live that way.

The differential here is "live in" versus "live after." A Christian sinning could be described as <u>acting after the flesh</u>, the idea of living after the flesh means that you've made the flesh your permanent zip code.

Unfortunately some Christians have!

I've discovered that the free grace message of the Bible must be predicated by the biblical truth. Every Christian on the face of the earth sins and continues in sin. To be operationally dead is to have no spirituality whatsoever. But don't be discouraged; if you read this and understood it, the Holy Spirit within you was just fed. I hope this book will be an encouragement to live after the spirit! ... (Colossians 2:6.)

FAITH ALONE.

Chapter 4

Repentance — Not in John's Gospel

The word repentance is a baffling word. What does it mean and is it part of the gospel? Is repentance in the rhetorical sense part of salvation? According to John—no. The words "repent" and "repentance," are not found in the Gospel of John, which is the only book in the Bible that deals exclusively with how a lost person is to be saved.

The word repentance is found in the New Testament many times but never as a prerequisite to being saved. The Gospel of John makes it clear what a person has to do in order to be saved.

BELIEVE!

John 3:15 — *That whosoever believeth in him should not perish, but have eternal life.*

You will hear preachers left and right adding repentance into the recipe for salvation and most do it out of ignorance or tradition. Repentance may accompany belief (Mark 1:15) but it is not always necessarily a synonym for belief. Despite all this, nobody can decide what repentance means. Some say it means to turn from sins, others say it means to stop sins or to contritely feel sorry for sins. But it doesn't matter because out of all the verses in the Bible that tell a person how to be saved, repentance is not included.

Acts 16:31 — *And they said, Believe on the Lord Jesus Christ, and thou shalt be saved, and thy house.*

Let's examine the books and scriptures of the New Testament (KJV) where the word 'repent' or 'repentance' are found.

Matthew ... 11 times.

Mark ... 4 times.

Luke ... 13 times.

Acts ... 10 times.

Romans ... 2 times.

2 Corinthians ... 4 times.

2 Timothy ... 1 time.

Hebrews ... 4 times.

2 Peter ... 1 time.

Revelation ... 5 times.

But never is it even mentioned in John's Gospel.

Read on...

John 3:16 — *For God so loved the world, that he gave his only begotten Son, that whosoever believeth in him should not perish, but have everlasting life.*

John 3:18 — *He that believeth on him is not condemned: but he that believeth not is condemned already, because he hath not believed in the name of the only begotten Son of God.*

John 3:36 — *He that believeth on the Son hath everlasting life: and he that believeth not the Son shall not see life; but the wrath of God abideth on him.*

John 5:24 — *Verily, verily, I say unto you, He that heareth my word, and believeth on him that sent me, hath everlasting life, and shall not come into condemnation; but is passed from death unto life.*

John 6:47 — *Verily, verily, I say unto you, He that believeth on me hath everlasting life.*

John 6:35 — *And Jesus said unto them, I am the bread of life: he that cometh to me shall never hunger; and he that believeth on me shall never thirst.*

John 7:38 — *He that believeth on me, as the scripture hath said, out of his belly shall flow rivers of living water.*

John 11:40 — *Jesus saith unto her, Said I not unto thee, that, if thou wouldest believe, thou shouldest see the glory of God?*

John never added repentance in any form to any of these gospel verses. Romans and Galatians are revisions of the gospel message in part for the churches of Rome and Galatia. They needed revision due to the rampant plague of Judaization, and the word repent is not found in Galatians at all either. We need to not make a big fuss as to what repent means in the salvific sense because it is not part of salvation. Faith/belief in Christ is all one has to do in order to be saved. This is the pure, unalloyed gospel.

I've frequented many churches where I have heard the preacher say things like, "take up your cross, or submit to Christ." Sure, I'm certain that his intention was pure, however his audience may not have been ready to hear a message that was strictly dealing with discipleship. I've even recently attended a church service where an entire family left in mid-sermon seemingly disgruntled. The message was themed: "take up your cross." For a seeking family who wants to know Christ and or what a person has to do in order to be saved, this was entirely antithetical to the gospel. Nobody understands how to carry their cross before they are saved. The sermon went something like this:

"Christ had to literally die on the cross for our sins, we don't have to do that ... *thank God*, but we do have to carry our cross and die to sin."

This intimates that we must turn from sins or stop sinning in, of, or by our own power. This is not the gospel, but is a hopeless rendition of the anti-gospel.

Imagine an addict of any kind wanting to be saved from the penalty of his sin. Wishful thinking had long ago unveiled to him that a surcease of the addiction itself was impossible but the hope of being delivered from the eternal consequences of the addiction is now the only thing being considered.

<u>What must I do to be saved?</u>

I may never overcome the addiction so how do I escape an eternity in hell?

The gospel is to realize that you are a sinner and obviously anyone who went to church because of an addiction has implicitly done that much, but now what? The only answer to this question is to believe in Christ for He alone is your only hope for salvation. But that's not what is typically being preached.

"Carry your cross! Submit to Christ." the preacher exclaims.

The poor addict construes it as "stop the addiction." He leaves abjectly, confused and now with the impression that he is unsavable! (beyond salvation.)

Now his opinion of God is horrific. Unless and until the gospel is initially preached at any service, the message of discipleship (take up your cross) will always be a full-bore disaster.

The gospel is faith alone in Christ alone.

Repentance has nothing to do with simple faith. It is a term for the church in most of its usages. It is not for the unbeliever in terms of salvation. Lewis Sperry Chafer described it as.

Quote:

"It is not turning from something to something; but rather turning to something from something." Unquote.

Here's more on repentance by Chafer in his Systematic Theology.

"The Gospel by John, which is written to present Christ as the object of faith unto eternal life, does not once employ the word *repentance*. The Fourth Gospel is incomplete and misleading if repentance must be accorded a place separate from, and independent of—believing. No thoughtful person would attempt to defend (repentance as a condition of salvation) against such odds, and those who have thus undertaken doubtless have done so without weighing the evidence or considering the untenable position which they assume." (3:376-77 Systematic Theology).

Lordship Salvationists have implied that repentance is found in the Johannine gospel in metaphor. They use Christic verses that suggest, "Follow me." But the context is to the disciples, the already saved followers of Christ.

John 21:19 — *This spake he, signifying by what death he should glorify God. And when he had spoken this, he saith unto him, Follow me.*

This is not demanding repentance. It doesn't make sense to suggest that a sequacious follower needs to make a sea change (repent) if they are already following their pilot.

The point of John's Gospel is found in:

John 20:30-31 — *And many other signs truly did Jesus in the presence of his disciples, which are not written in this book: But these are written, that ye might <u>believe</u> that Jesus is the Christ, the Son of God; and that <u>believing</u> ye might have life through his name.*

How many times did you see the word "repent" in that latter verse?"

NONE!

Another interesting thing about repentance is that Judas Iscariot repented and he wasn't saved.

Matthew 27:3 — *Then Judas, which had betrayed him, when he saw that he was condemned, repented himself, and brought again the thirty pieces of silver to the chief priests and elders.*

John 17:12 — *While I was with them in the world, I kept them in thy name: those that thou gavest me I have kept, and none of them is lost, but the son of perdition; that the scripture might be fulfilled.*

If, in this case where a contrite act of repentance didn't save, how are we to believe that Christians today are called to repent? No amount of sorrow for sin, turning from sin or any other form of repentance is necessary for salvation. Judas went to hell because he didn't trust in Christ for salvation. If repentance means to turn from unbelief then it is used correctly. Turning from unbelief is to believe the gospel.

Faith Alone. THE WAY TO CHRIST.

Chapter 5

How Many Sins?

The law condemns the best person; grace justifies the worst.

C. I. Scofield.

Psalm 40:12 — *For innumerable evils have compassed me about:* mine iniquities *have taken hold upon me, so that I am not able to look up; they are more than* the hairs of mine head: *therefore my heart faileth me.*

What about if we keep on sinning?

What about people that say that if you keep on sinning, you will no longer be saved. Let me preface by saying that to keep on sinning is not fun. It leaves you with chronic depression, spiritual brokenness, monetary indigence, addictions, self-embarrassment, aloofness, and unending guilt. It also saps ones fervor for praying due to self-centered shame. So don't think that I'm freeing people to sin. I'm just being realistic.

We sin all the time. To think, preach or deem otherwise it to be ensconced in self-deception and ignorance. (Romans 7:11.)

Hamartiology is the study of sin. Here's the general historic understanding of hamartiology.

Most breeds of hamartiological insight subscribe to the Augustinian doctrine of original sin which was taught by the

Apostle Paul in Romans 5:12-19 and further popularized by, hence the eponym, Saint Augustine. He taught that all the descendants of the Adamic gene pool were invariably guilty of Adam's sin without their own personal choice.

This is correct; I do believe however that we must account for our own sins inherited from Adam. To deny the doctrine of original sin is to embrace the heresy of Palagianism or Arminianism.

That's why we need Christ.

The reason I'm writing about hamartiology is because most people would make dishonest hamartiologists. In layman terms, what I'm alluding to here is that most people don't understand the severity or vastness of sin, namely their own sinfulness.

We not only sin but we are sinFULL!

Luke 5:8 — *When Simon Peter saw it, he fell down at Jesus' knees, saying, Depart from me; for I am a <u>sinful</u> man, O Lord.*

I find that the enlightened Christians when it comes to sin, normally humbly confess to being outright wretches. No verses in the Bible speak more colorfully to me than verses on man's inherent depravity. Daniel 9:5-15.

By saying that you can't be saved or that you aren't saved if you keep on sinning, is insulting the Savior.

Scripture says in:

1 John 2:2 — *And he is the propitiation for our sins: and not for ours only, but also for the sins of the whole world.*

That means that he died for every sin ever committed and for the commissions of sin for every person that has ever existed, and ever will exist. So how many sins did He die for? Let's just get out our calculator. Let's round this off to the Billions. Let's say that from the beginning of time, until the end of time, approximately 100, 000, 000, 000 (one-hundred billion) people lived and died and entered into eternity. Now, this is an understatement but let's surmise that each person throughout his or her lifetime committed one million sins. That's a gross underestimation if we are to be honest.

Now let's say that you, one individual Christian, after being saved, commits roughly 35,000 sins before you die. Are you telling me that a God — who has promised to save the sins of the entire world — which could hypothetically estimate to be 100,000,000,000,000,000 sins, can't cover your 35,000? That's one hundred quadrillion sins by the way. If Christ can cover that many sins, wouldn't it be insulting to Him to think or to say that he can't cover whatever sins you continue to commit after you are saved?

Once again, I'm not condoning sin. Because for every sin committed Christ bore more sufferance for us. It's high time we stopped allowing the opponents of free grace to have any more room for the outspreading of their loutish, heretical drivel that affects the minds and hearts of the true Solafidian believers.

Here's another way to look at sin.

So many people want to look at sin as an action. Someone fornicates or gossips and we want to condemn them. Keep in mind these sins have been deemed as actions. Onetime events that happen over and over again. Singular events if you will. But that's not what sin is. Sin is an inherent condition. The acts of sin are results of this condition. For instance, pride. Pride is not an action it is a condition. Arrogant bragging or a self-righteous quip are results of pride. But so many Christians want to gauge sin as actions thus condemning one another for the recurrence and continuation of such actions.

You can't do that because sin is one condition that produces many ramifying actions. But since so many Christians want to look at sin as actions, ... let's humor them.

If they want to see certain sins as actions, like murder, forni-cation, stealing, lying, etc, then we must look at all sins as actions—in all equity. How do we do this? First, we must establish what the quickest sins are. Lust, cussing, name-calling. But let's choose one. A good example would be a cussword. It only takes a second. So if we cuss twelve times in twelve seconds, we've committed twelve sins. Pretty logical way of gauging sin. Don't you think?

Let's say that a person is full of pride. How do we actionify (my neologism) pride? Well, we've established that one can fill up twelve seconds with twelve sins (cusswords) so it must be quanti-fied by the second. I could take this to a numerically deeper level but that's not the point. Anyway. Twelve individual cusswords is no different than twelve individual acts of pride. So if a person is prideful for ten minutes he has committed 600 sins.

Why can't you say that he has committed one sin thus meas-uring sin in ten-minute increments? Because each second was the "act of pride". It wouldn't be fair to cuss 600 times; onetime per second and then just call it one sin. Because that would separate action from condition and we can't do that if one wants to judge the act of, for example, fornication that way.

So if a person is prideful for an entire hour they are guilty of 3,600 sins. If they are prideful for an entire, wakeful twelve-hour day, they are guilty of 43,200 sins. So who's guiltier? The fornica-tor who's committed one sin or the prideful man who's committed 43,200 sins. But what about counting the seconds of the longevity of fornication and enumerating his sins in that manner?

You can't; you've already declared that fornication is a singular action. Pride could only be reasoned this way by making it into actions, fornication according to the mindset of viewing sin as "actions," must be declared as one action.

Then you'd be forced to say, "You can't gauge sin like this." I know. That's my initial point. Sin can't be viewed as actions, but only as a condition. And that being the case, everyone has it and everyone is equally guilty. If you really want to see sins this way then a prideful teetotaler is guiltier than a humble drunk!

Now let's look at other conditions and actionify them. Self-righteousness. It can't be the action; it can only engender sinful acts like a judgmental harangue or the repudiation of another sinner. Let's say that you stay self-righteous and prideful everyday, all day long. You've got this sanctimonious air that's inclined to judge others for being carnal. Throughout the course of the day you rant about 50 times due to your self-righteousness. Fifty actuated sins added to 43,200. And that's just self-righteousness. If you want to add that to pride you've now committed 86,450 sins. If you go an entire week starting from Monday remaining in these two actions, then before you make it to church on Sunday you will have committed 518,700 plus sins just in pride and self-righteousness alone.

Now this is a radical way of understanding sin, so maybe we shouldn't measure sin as actions and trust the benefit of our intellect by realizing that sin is an ineluctable condition. All have it and all are equally guilty. Romans 3:22-23. Galatians 3:22. Ecclesiastes 7:20. 1 Kings 8:46. Isaiah 64:6, 1 John 1:8-10, Psalms 51:5. Proverbs 20:9. Psalm 58:3.

The wicked are estranged from the womb: they go astray as soon as they be born, speaking lies.

Faith alone. THE WAY TO CHRIST.

Chapter 6

Faith Plus Christ's Work

Q: Do you believe in faith alone or faith plus works?

The protestant might say faith alone. The Catholic may reply with faith plus works.

So, what's my reply?

My reply is: faith plus Christ's work. Some people, both Protestants and Catholics have a problem with faith in Christ alone. And the reason for this is because they think it is too easy. There has to be something more man is prone to believe. Faith alone seems flimsy, insubstantial, and vaporous. To add a little substance to their doctrine they include water baptism or sacraments or other forms of good works. It gives their ecclesiology something to cling to.

"Faith alone, no way, there's got to be more to it."

And there is; there's a lot more to it. If you put faith alone in a tree or a magic ball then faith alone would be absurd. But a tree and a magic ball have no power to save anyone. Faith alone in Christ is different. Christ is the object of our faith so if you need something substantial to cling to—cling to Him.

I still don't like this, someone may be thinking. There has to be something else that has to happen to accompany faith.

There is!

There's a lot more that has to happen. *But I thought you said faith alone was enough.* It's enough in terms of what <u>man</u> has to do, but that doesn't negate the fact that so much more has (had) to happen. So what else is it that has to happen?

Scourging, being spat upon and scorned, public humiliation, being pelted by sharps rocks, having spikes forcibly driven into your wrists, having your flesh ripped apart and your bones disjointed, bleeding every last drop of blood you have, being nailed to a rugged cross, abandoned from your heavenly father, living a sinless life, having a spear thrust into your side, dying, having the sins of the entire world imputed to you, being condemned in the flesh, being buried and then resurrected three days later. That's what else has to happen. Fortunately, for us, it already happened to Christ and we don't have to undergo any of it.

So, the next time someone says that faith alone is too simple whether it be Catholic or Protestant, remind him or her that faith is not alone; faith includes everything else Christ did for us. It also excludes anything and everything we try to do for God but help-lessly fall short at our best attempt.

So many people are bent to say that faith must include our good works for it to be real faith. Wrong! Faith does include <u>the perfect work</u> of Christ for us. Nothing we do could ever compare to that. There's so much more than faith alone when it comes to the Christian life. For salvation faith alone is it. But for spiritual growth, there's a plethora of things we should do. Man mustn't confuse sanctification with justification.

If all a person wanted was justification then all he has to do is have faith in Christ. (Romans 3:28.) That's easier than breathing. But if a person wants to know how to be sanctified which is actively progressive then there's a whole lifetime of things to be done. So, do I believe in faith alone or in faith plus works?

My answer again is ... I believe it is ... *faith plus Christ's fin-ished work at Calvary!*

Faith alone. THE WAY TO CHRIST.

Chapter 7

Working For Salvation NEVER Works!

Titus 3:5 — *Not by works of righteousness which we have done, but according to his mercy he saved us, by the washing of regeneration, and renewing of the Holy Ghost.*

"For those that accuse me or other free grace writers of..."

"License to sin!"

"Cheap grace!"

"Antinomianism!"

My counter response to such people in keeping with their doctrine is.

"No grace!"

"Self-confidence!"

"You're back under the law!"

The Judaizers were trying to work for their salvation but this doesn't work.

Romans 9:30-33.

30—What shall we say then? That the Gentiles, which followed not after righteousness, have attained to righteousness, even the righteousness which is of faith.

The Gentiles in this verse attained righteousness by faith. But Israel, or the Jews, were adamantly insistent on attaining righteousness by the law. Some may even have been thinking that, "this is not working ... we must become even more righteous." But read the next verse.

31—But Israel, which followed after the law of righteousness, hath not attained to the law of righteousness.

They followed the law and this verse affirms that they hadn't yet attained righteousness. It wasn't that they weren't good enough or didn't obey the law amply enough because nobody does; it was that the law couldn't bring righteousness. (Hebrews 10:1, Galatians 2:21.) We'll get there.

32—Wherefore? Because they sought it not by faith, but as it were by the works of the law. For they stumbled at that stumblingstone;

33—As it is written, Behold, I lay in Sion a stumblingstone and rock of offence: and whosoever believeth on him shall not be ashamed.

Galatians 2:21 — *I do not frustrate the grace of God: for if righteousness come by the law, then Christ is dead in vain.*

Righteousness does not come by obeying the law no matter how hard you try to obey it. Self-righteous people have missed the boat when it comes to justification.

Romans 10:3 — *For they being ignorant of God's righteousness, and going about to establish their <u>own righteousness</u>, have not submitted themselves unto the righteousness of God.*

Deuteronomy 6:25 — *And if we are careful to obey all this law before the LORD our God, as he has commanded us, that will be our righteousness.*

This is not God's imputed righteousness that comes by faith alone, Philippians 3:9. It is man's righteousness, which is worthless, Romans 10:3.

The legalists, Judaizers, Pharisees, or anyone else that tries to put Christians under the bondage of the law have not submitted to the righteousness of God, which is not submission at all, but rather a simple acceptance through faith in Christ. The reason for this book and the overemphasis I'm belaboring is because most people believe in free grace in theory but not in practice.

We are free in Christ. Free to serve Him and even free from sin in that the penalty has been removed. But keep in mind; sinning freely may be fun at first but when all is said and done, it is a disaster. We can do it and still be saved and some even do a lot of it. But if you are a Child of God you will pay for your sins in both this life and the next (chastisement, loss of rewards). What I'm trying to say is that sin stinks!

We sin because we are sinners; we are not sinners because we sin. Keeping the law as a Christian can do one of two things. It can safeguard us from peril and also expose us to our true depraved natures that reveal to us that the law is not the least bit keepable without the ministrations of the Holy Spirit—and still at best we fail miserably.

This subset is not to undermine good works. The doctrine of good works is only heresy when contingent upon our eternal salvation or justification. The doctrine of good works in keeping with progressive sanctification is the only platform by which we must embrace and uphold our obedience to God. We should do good works because we are saved not in order to be saved.

1 Corinthians 15:34 — *Awake to righteousness, and sin not; for some have not the knowledge of God: I speak this to your shame.*

In other words, know that you have been declared righteous because of what Christ did for you! Working for salvation never works because salvation is a free gift. (Romans 5:15, 16,18. Romans 6:23. John 4:10. Ephesians 2:8-9, 3:7.)

After we have received salvation freely, our good works, not mandatory however, are rich, admirable and will be rewarded in heaven.

Faith Alone. THE WAY TO CHRIST.

Chapter 8

Christ In Isaiah

Our standing in Christ rests on God's word. Isaiah illustrates each facet of Jesus through prophecy. This subset demonstrates how every nominal characteristic of Jesus can be found in scriptural order.

Isaiah 7:14, prophesies the birth of Christ.

Therefore the Lord himself shall give you a sign; Behold, a virgin shall conceive, and bear a son, and shall call his name Immanuel.

He is further expounded as the Son of God and given five of His many names.

Isaiah 9:6 — *For unto us a child is born, unto us a son is given: and the government shall be upon his shoulder: and his name shall be called Wonderful, Counsellor, The mighty God, The everlasting Father, The Prince of Peace.*

Wonderful.

Counselor.

The mighty God.

The everlasting Father.

The Prince of peace.

Jesus is knowledge and wisdom, council and might.

Isaiah 11:2 — *And the spirit of the LORD shall rest upon him, the spirit of wisdom and understanding, the spirit of counsel and might, the spirit of knowledge and of the fear of the LORD.*

Jesus is our righteousness.

Isaiah 32:1 — *Behold, a king shall reign in righteousness, and princes shall rule in judgment.*

Jesus is silence.

Isaiah 42:2 — *He shall not cry, nor lift up, nor cause his voice to be heard in the street.*

Jesus is meekness.

Isaiah 42:3 — *A bruised reed shall he not break, and the smoking flax shall he not quench: he shall bring forth judgment unto truth.*

Jesus never fails.

Isaiah 42:4 — *He shall not fail nor be discouraged, till he have set judgment in the earth: and the isles shall wait for his law.*

Jesus is radiance.

Isaiah 42:6 — *I the LORD have called thee in righteousness, and will hold thine hand, and will keep thee, and give thee for a covenant of the people, for a light of the Gentiles.*

Jesus Christ is our liberator.

Isaiah 42:7 — *To open the blind eyes, to bring out the prisoners from the prison, and them that sit in darkness out of the prison house.*

Jesus is the arm of God.

Isaiah 53:1 — *Who hath believed our report? and to whom is the arm of the LORD revealed?*

Jesus is compassion.

Isaiah 53:4 — *Surely he hath borne our griefs, and carried our sorrows: yet we did esteem him stricken, smitten of God, and afflicted.*

Jesus suffered for us revealing that He is the only way.

Isaiah 53:5 — *But he was wounded for our transgressions, he was bruised for our iniquities: the chastisement of our peace was upon him; and with his stripes we are healed.*

Jesus is the Saviour to all who will have Him.

Isaiah 53:6 — *All we like sheep have gone astray; we have turned every one to his own way; and the LORD hath laid on him the iniquity of us all.*

Jesus was a lamb to be slaughtered.

Isaiah 53:7 — *He was oppressed, and he was afflicted, yet he opened not his mouth: he is brought as a lamb to the slaughter, and as a sheep before her shearers is dumb, so he openeth not his mouth.*

Our sins crucified Him.

Isaiah 53:8 — *He was taken from prison and from judgment: and who shall declare his generation? for he was cut off out of the land of the living: for the transgression of my people was he stricken.*

Jesus was sinless.

Isaiah 53:9 — *And he made his grave with the wicked, and with the rich in his death; because he had done no violence, neither was any deceit in his mouth.*

God was pleased with making Christ a sacrifice for us.

Isaiah 53:10 — *Yet it pleased the LORD to bruise him; he hath put him to grief: when thou shalt make his soul an offering for sin, he shall see his seed, he shall prolong his days, and the pleasure of the LORD shall prosper in his hand.*

Jesus bore all sins, past, present and future.

Isaiah 53:11 — *He shall see of the travail of his soul, and shall be satisfied: by his knowledge shall my righteous servant justify many; for he shall bear their iniquities.*

Jesus is our intercessor.

Isaiah 53:12 — *Therefore will I divide him a portion with the great, and he shall divide the spoil with the strong; because he hath poured out his soul unto death: and he was numbered with the transgressors; and he bare the sin of many, and made intercession for the transgressors.*

He did all this for us and all we must do is receive Him as our Saviour by faith!

JESUS SAVES!

****

Isaian Salvation.

The Fourfold Message of Salvation.

Isaiah 45:21-22 — *Tell ye, and bring them near; yea, let them take counsel together: who hath declared this from ancient time? who hath told it from that time? have not I the LORD? and there is no God else beside me; a just God and a Saviour; there is none beside me.*

Look unto me, and be ye saved, all the ends of the earth: for I am God, and there is none else.

Let's focus on verse 22.

We could break it down to explain every aspect of salvation, the simplicity, inclusivity, Christ-aloneness and even security.

Salvation is in Jesus. (I am God and there is none else.)

Salvation is for everyone. (All the ends of the earth.)

Salvation is by simple faith. (Look unto me.)

Salvation is certain and secure. (And be ye saved.)

Faith alone. The way to Christ.

Chapter 9

Covenant Of Grace

Free grace according to Chafer and Dispensationalism.
Free grace says: I have blessed you, now be good.

Covenant theology says: I'll be good to get the blessings.

"If heaven were no better than just reading Lewis Sperry Chafer for 24 hours a day than that would be fine with me. Fortunately, it will be myriad times better."

Matt.

Statistically Arminians convert to Calvinism at a high percentage. Calvinists convert to Arminianism at a lesser rate, but for the most part nobody converts from dispensationalism to anything.

Lewis Sperry Chafer

...Paraphrased.

Understanding Dispensationalism.

What is it?

Wikipedia says:

Dispensationalism is a Christian theological view of history and Biblical interpretation that became popular during the 1800's and early 1900's and is held today by many conservative Protestants. It supplies an interpretive grid for understanding the flow of the Bible as a whole, and it is frequently contrasted with opposing views such as Covenant Theology, where the fundamental difference is the relationship between the nations of Israel and Judah on the one hand and the Christian church on the other.

What is my definition? Well, a dispensation is how the Bible divides church ages.

Here are the seven dispensations in chronological order.

Innocence. (Genesis 1-3.)

Conscience. (Genesis 4-6.)

Human government. (Genesis 7-11.)

Promise. (Genesis 12.)

Law. (Exodus 20.)

Grace. (Romans.)

Millennial kingdom. (Revelation 20.)

Dispensationalism is the idea that we, the church, are in the dispensation of grace hence the covenants of grace and law are to be totally separated and distinct. Israel is not the church and is to be referred to in the dispensations of promise, law and millennial kingdom. I will not go into much detail about the church and Israel being distinctly separated because of my ineptitude on the subject but I will go over some of the reasons that free grace theology is highly contingent upon having a proper dispensationalist viewpoint. There are many types of Dispensationalisms.

I will go over some of those in due time. The reason I'm emphasizing Dispensationalism is because the importance in holding to it doctrinally is of the essence in free grace theology.

Lewis Sperry Chafer writes concerning the retardation of Christ's resurrection is the obvious stance of any antidispensationalistic view. A better way to describe such a stance is to give you the antithesis of Dispensationalism, which is any form of covenant theology or covenantism. In laymen terms, it's the admixture of grace and law.

Here are the words of Lewis Sperry Chafer.

Retarded Resurrection. As traced by Covenant theologians, the death of Christ is given a place of large significance but His resurrection is accounted as little more than something for His own personal convenience, His necessary return from the sphere of death back to the place which He occupied before. In other words, as viewed by Covenant theologians, there is practically no doctrinal significance to Christ's resurrection (and me identified with Him!) That Christ by resurrection became what in Himself He had not been before—the federal Head of a wholly new order (creation) of beings and these the primary divine objective, as this is set forth in the Pauline Epistles—cannot be incorporated into a system of which the cherished and distinctive feature is one unchangeable divine purpose from Adam to the end of time.

Back to me.

Here's my amateurish take on Dispensationalism. The church and Israel must be distinct in order to differentiate between grace and law. Israel represents those under law symbolically for the purpose of such a distinction. We are in the dispensation of grace not to have bragging rights so that we can feel like we have been auspiciously begat in the ideal dispensation and those that dispensationally predated us were unfortunate by being under the law. No. The church is always in the dispensation of grace. If we had been in the dispensation of promise or human government for instance, we would still be under grace.

The only reason we have the dispensations delineated in the chronological order that we are familiar with is to show us that the church in any dispensation is always distinct from Israel. The whole reason that Israel is in the seventh dispensation is because they will represent no need for grace. Israel will be in God's kingdom where his eternal grace will be poured upon all believers, but this is not salvific grace, this is heavenly or ethereal grace. We, the church, are in the dispensation of grace now simply to exemplify what grace is and the dire need for it.

The distinction between the covenant of grace and the covenant of the law is the only way to grasp the freeness of grace. Therefore any admixture of grace and law in our doctrine, theology or practice is heresy.

This is difficult to understand so let me give you some renowned dispensationalists interpretations on Dispensationalism, starting with C. I. Scofield along with a few of the different types of Dispensationalism.

Quote:

A dispensation is a period of time during which man is tested in respect of obedience to some specific revelation of the will of God. Seven such dispensations are distinguished in Scripture." A look at the etymology of the English word also gives insight to the understanding of this word. The English word dispensation is an Anglicized form of the Latin dispensation, which the Vulgate uses to translate the Greek word. Three principle ideas are connected to the meaning of the English word: The action of dealing out or distributing; the action of administering, ordering, or managing; the system by which things are administered; and the action of dispensing with some requirement. For our theological purposes the word is defined by the same dictionary as "a stage in a progressive revelation, expressly adapted to the needs of a particular nation or period of time..."

Unquote.

Here are descriptions of two types of Dispensationalism.

Neo-Dispensationalism.

According to Miles J Stanford, this form of Dispensationalism is an oxymoronic misnomer.

His words: Neo-Dispensationalism is a compromise toward Covenantism. Its progenitors are Dr. Craig A. Blaising, Dr. Darrell L. Bock, and in absentia, Dr. Robert L. Saucy. It was spawned in the Chaferless milieu of Dallas Theological Seminary.

What can Neo-Dispensationalism do to you? It can bring you down to earth with a thud, and relentlessly grind and ground you. It can make you a partaker of Israel's comparatively paltry New Covenant, and thereby subject you to the laws of its Sermon on the Mount, and Millennial Kingdom. It can reduce you to a hybrid—part Christian and part reconstructed kingdom Jew.

Pauline Dispensationalism is according to Miles J. Stanford simply a system according to Paul's teaching.

Quote:

This is our position by virtue of our baptism (by the Spirit) into Christ, and it is on the basis of this positional fact that Paul writes to the Colossians: *"If (since)ye, then, be risen with Christ, seek those things which are above, where Christ sitteth on the right hand of God. Set your affection on things above, not on things on the earth. For ye died, and your life is hid with Christ in God."* (Col. 3:1-3).

Unquote.

I'm simply defining it as this. To deny Dispensationalism is to suggest that we are to be dealt with by God in a manner other than grace. Had we been born again by faith in Christ alone in any other dispensation, that dispensation would be of grace. The idea is to show us that we, the church are in grace, and Israel, The Jews, who haven't yet accepted Christ as the Messiah are still under the law only because they choose to be by refusing immiscible grace.

I've heard many Christians say that salvation by grace was really simple and by implication were suggesting that I didn't need to read a Lewis Sperry Chafer book to understand it. But some of us are just wired differently and have an insatiable predilection for convolution, that being my problem.

The free grace message IS simple! Forget all the big, theological words.

Ephesians 2:8-9.
For by grace are ye saved through faith; and that not of yourselves: it is the gift of God: Not of works, lest any man should boast.

The dispensational kingdom of heaven.

Why Judaism doesn't work.

Judaism is totally anti-dispensationalistic. Only Matthew uses the terminology "kingdom of heaven". Why, because it is Judaistic in its connotation. According to Judaism, you are still under the mosaic law and if one were to ask how to enter the kingdom of Heaven the Judaistic response would be Mathew 5:20. The kingdom of heaven (earthly kingdom) is entered by one's own righteousness exceeding the Pharisees.

The kingdom of God is the all-encompassing eternal kingdom much different than the kingdom of heaven and according to dispensationalist Christianity; it is entered only by a new birth, which is freely attained by grace through faith. John 3:1-16. Judaism's kingdom of heaven offers no hope for either Israel or the gentiles unless they can surpass the pharisaical standard, which no one can. Furthermore, the kingdom of God is an all-inclusive offer to both the Jew and the Gentile. Romans 1:16.

For more on this subject see my subset entitled: Kingdom of Heaven vs. Kingdom of God.

The Abrahamic covenant versus the Palestinian covenant.

Genesis 12:1-3 — *Now the LORD had said unto Abram, Get thee out of thy country, and from thy kindred, and from thy father's house, unto a land that I will shew thee: And I will make of thee a great nation, and I will bless thee, and make thy name great; and thou shalt be a blessing: And I will bless them that bless thee, and curse him that curseth thee: and in thee shall all families of the earth be blessed.*

This covenant was dispensational and completely by grace.

Genesis 15:6 — *And he believed in the LORD; and he counted it to him for righteousness.*

This runs in stark contrast with the Palestinian covenant, which offers no optimistic desiderata. A great nation, a blessed nation, a great name. These are all auspicious aspects of this covenant by grace. But look at what the Palestinian covenant has to offer.

Deuteronomy 28:65-67 — *And among these nations shalt thou find <u>no ease</u>, neither shall the sole of thy foot have <u>rest</u>: but the LORD shall give thee there a <u>trembling heart</u>, and <u>failing of eyes</u>, and <u>sorrow of mind</u>: And thy life shall <u>hang in doubt</u> before thee; and thou shalt <u>fear day and night</u>, and shalt have <u>none assurance of thy life</u>: In the morning thou shalt say, Would God it were even! and at even thou shalt say, Would God it were morning! for the <u>fear of thine</u> heart wherewith thou shalt <u>fear</u>, and for the sight of thine eyes which thou shalt see.*

This is diacritically opposed to the Abrahamic covenantal promise. I've underlined all the negative punctilios of this horrible covenant.

Fear. Doubt. No assurance. Sounds like the mantras of the works-Salvationists.

It says in Jeremiah that nobody kept this legalistic covenant anyway.

Jeremiah 31:32 — *Not according to the covenant that I made with their fathers in the day that I took them by the hand to bring them out of the land of Egypt; which my covenant they brake, although I was an husband unto them, saith the LORD.*

Also.

Hebrews 8:9 — *Not according to the covenant that I made with their fathers in the day when I took them by the hand to lead them out of the land of Egypt; because they <u>continued not in my covenant</u>, and I regarded them not, saith the Lord.*

See the inherent pointlessness in trying to keep any covenantal laws.

Chafer quotes:

"How many men have been led to a saving knowledge of a crucified and risen Savior by calling on them to repent for the kingdom of heaven is at hand?"

Well, to answer him is: NONE!

The dispensationalist's gospel.

It has been rumored that dispensationalism bisects, pluralizes or gives two gospels—in other words, two ways to be saved. This is just unwitting malignity. The gospel of repentance is found in:

Matthew 4:17 — *From that time Jesus began to preach, and to say, Repent: for the kingdom of heaven is at hand.*

Repentance was for Israel for reasons of revival, restoration, not for eternal salvation. Whether every Israelite was individually saved here is immaterial because Israel as a whole needed revival much like some churches of modernity.

This type of repentance is not salvific. The only kind of repentance a lost person can produce is to change his mind (metanoia) about his sins and ask to be saved by grace through faith. A continuance of sinfulness has nothing to do with such a change of mind. So we've distinguished two things. The gospel of repentance is for Israel holistically and the gospel of grace is for everyone. (John 6:47, 3:16, Romans 1:16, Acts 16:31.)

What about forgiveness from a dispensationalist viewpoint?

Some anti-dispensationalists would add the work of forgiveness as a qualification for salvation. But they do err not knowing the proper interpretation of the scripture, nor the power of God.

Matthew 6:14-15 — *For if ye forgive men their trespasses, your heavenly Father will also forgive you: But if ye forgive not men their trespasses, neither will your Father forgive your trespasses.*

They will say that if a man harbors unforgiveness in his heart toward his brother than God has not or will not forgive them. Which is true. But we must keep in mind that there are two types of forgiveness. Divine, forensic forgiveness, which is part of salvation and is permeated in adoption, imputation, justification, redemption, reconciliation and ultimately glorification.

Colossians 2:13 — *And you, being dead in your sins and the uncircumcision of your flesh, hath he quickened together with him, having forgiven you all trespasses.*

This is a done deal! Not something subject to change, accrue or lay prey to any added qualifications.

The other kind of forgiveness is filial or household forgiveness.

This is a personal issue between man and God and has nothing whatsoever to do with man's justification before God. This is a 1 John 1:9 issue that is linked to sanctification.

Ephesians 4:32 — *And be ye kind one to another, tenderhearted, forgiving one another, even as God for Christ's sake hath forgiven you.*

Because God has forgiven us completely upon our first moment of faith, scripture exhorts us to forgive one another. Don't let anyone make forgiveness a qualification for salvation.

That is just adding works yet done in a more subtle and deceptive manner. Dispensationalism is practically the only way to understand free grace. So, how do you know if you are a dispensationalist?

If you are trusting in the Blood of Jesus apart from works for your salvation, you are a dispensationalist. Historically, it was someone who understood the Sabbath to be the first day of the week as opposed to being the last. Think about it. You rest in God's grace first so that you may work the rest of the week long as opposed to trying to work for your salvation so that grace at the last day of the week could be attained. This heresy is the crux of covenant theology.

Faith Alone. THE WAY TO CHRIST.

Chapter 10

Obedience Unto Faith

Romans 10:16 — *But they have not all obeyed the gospel. For Esaias saith, Lord, who hath believed our report?*

There's so much talk about obedience in Christian circles. Obey the law! True faith is obedient they say. Faith without works is dead. I've heard all the jargon and it is almost to the point of silliness. The Bible makes it crystal clear that all a person has to do to be saved is to believe on Christ for salvation. People have taken scriptures out of context in order to add to this simple truth and some of the scriptures they use are Romans 1:5, 16:26. I've heard a preacher say that faith and obedience are one and the same and always accompany one another. This is simply not true. Obedience to God's words should follow from faith but it doesn't always. John 12:42-43.

Let's look at these verses and see if they in fact make the faith and obedience nexus legitimate.

Romans 1:5 — *By whom we have received grace and apostle-ship, for obedience to the faith among all nations, for his name.*

False teachers try to smuggle in works by implying that this verse demands obedience. The problem with this conjecture is that it says obedience unto faith, not obedience to the law. Galatians 3:21-22 makes it clear that faith alone excludes the law.

Is the law then against the promises of God? God forbid: for if there had been a law given which could have given life, verily righteousness should have been by the law.

But the scripture hath concluded all under sin, that the promise by faith of Jesus Christ might be <u>given to them that believe</u>.

The other verse they may use is:

Romans 16:26 — *But now is made manifest, and by the scriptures of the prophets, according to the commandment of the everlasting God, made known to all nations for the obedience of faith.*

Obedience unto faith simply means to believe the gospel. Faith alone in Christ alone.

Obedience in the Greek here is Hupakoe, which means to listen attentively. Faith cometh by hearing. (Romans 10:17.) Obedience unto faith is simply to hear the gospel message and then believe it for eternal life.

The other verses people might use to convolve faith plus obedience is:

2 Thessalonians 1:8 — *In flaming fire taking vengeance on them that know not God, and that obey not the gospel of our Lord Jesus Christ.*

1 Peter 4:17 — *For the time is come that judgment must begin at the house of God: and if it first begin at us, what shall the end be of them that obey not the gospel of God?*

"Obey not" in the Greek is Apeitheo, which literally means disbelieve. Obey is a synonym for believe in this verse. Obeying the gospel is simply believing that Christ died for your sins.

In Isaiah the gospel is prophesied in the following verse.

Isaiah 61:1 — *The Spirit of the Lord GOD is upon me; because the LORD hath anointed me to preach good tidings unto the meek; he hath sent me to bind up the brokenhearted, to proclaim liberty to the captives, and the opening of the prison to them that are bound.*

"Good tidings" means good news. There wouldn't be any thing good about a gospel message that required obedience. A child understands this. Any deeply ingrained sinner understands this. When the Bible says: obedience unto faith, it means just that, believing on the Lord Jesus Christ for salvation. Nothing less, nothing more.

Faith alone is the only way to Christ.

Chapter 11

Perseverance of the Saints Refuted

Perseverance in the faith is a great thing until it becomes either a demand or qualifying evidence for salvation—such conditions make even the most commendable endeavor to persevere a living heresy in effect.

Matt.

Some will try to refute this doctrine under the Arminian guise. But I will refute it under the free grace guise without stepping into the muddy territory of the Arminian heresy. The doctrine of perseverance of the saints traditionally is this. Every believer will persevere in good works until he dies. Those who don't persevere, like backsliders that is, prove to not be true believers. First of all, this doctrine is not commendable when viewed this way, for it is a satanic heresy.

For one, you have to try to define what it means to "persevere."

Some may say that the Bible describes perseverance with terms like "overcome" or "endure" or "be faithful to the end." they twist scripture out of context in order to sell their poisonous doctrine.

Let's take a look at a scripture that a proponent of P.O.T.S. might use.

Revelation 3:21 — *To him that overcometh will I grant to sit with me in my throne, even as I also overcame, and am set down with my Father in his throne.*

Overcoming in this passage is directly connected to eternal rewards.

Reigning with Christ will be a reward for overcomers; this has nothing to do with entering heaven, which is by faith alone. The proponents of P.O.T.S. make perseverance a prerequisite for salvation even when they suggest that perseverance is just an inevitable result of salvation.

That's a deceptive subtlety.

Saying that something must result from something in order to know that you have something (salvation) requires the result.

It would be like me saying that I'm going to give to a little boy a twenty-pound dumbbell, and because I've given it to him it therefore means that he will automatically workout and gain muscle mass. Two years later, because he only used it once, (didn't persevere) he has the same musculature as he did when I gave him the dumbbell. Would it be logical to think that he never <u>received</u> it?

Ridiculous!

What somebody does with grace has nothing to do with its reception.

Do all true Christians persevere?

No!

2 Timothy 4:10 — *For Demas hath forsaken me, having loved this present world, and is departed unto Thessalonica; Crescens to Galatia, Titus unto Dalmatia.*

Bob Wilkin puts it this way.

"Demas was a trusted member of the apostle Paul's ministry team. Paul said of him, "Epaphras, my fellow prisoner greets you, as do Mark, Aristarchus, *Demas*, Luke, my fellow laborers." (Philemon 23-24). Demas is even mentioned before Luke, author of Luke and Acts! Paul mentions him again in Colossians 4:14, also in a positive light."

So Demas clearly was a true Christian and yet he represents a non-perseverer.

Paul later describes Demas along with many other people as fellowlabourers.

Philemon 1:24 — *Marcus, Aristarchus, Demas, Lucas, my fellow labourers.*

Some may try to say that Demas was no different than Judas in that he wasn't a true brother, but the scripture never describes Demas as a *son of perdition* or a *devil.*

John 6:70 — *Jesus answered them, Have not I chosen you twelve, and one of you is a devil?*

That's referring to Judas who wasn't even saved. Scripture only says that Demas forsook the ministry. It doesn't say that he became lost, proved he wasn't really saved or anything the proponents of P.O.T.S. may say. P.O.T.S. is of the devil and manmade with no adherence to the true hermeneutics of scripture. Am I saying it is a bad thing to persevere in the faith? No. I encourage it. But to demand it or suggest that all true believers will persevere and to redefine what perseverance means is perverting the gospel and unbiblical. The Bible speaks many times of people who weren't persevering or that didn't persevere.

Luke 8:13 — *They on the rock are they, which, when they hear, receive the word with joy; and these have no root, which for a while believe, and in time of temptation fall away.*

Receiving the word with joy denotes that they were saved; however because of their lack of fortitude (having no root), they fell away due to temptation. You may say that this sower was not a true believer but let's look at what the Bible says.

This same sower is described in Matthew 13:5-6.

Some fell upon stony places, where they had not much earth: and forthwith they sprung up, because they had no deepness of earth: And when the sun was up, they were scorched; and because they had no root, they withered away.

The latter part reveals that because the sower had no root, the pleasures and temptations of this world caused his faith to wither away, but he did in the beginning produce some fruit.

<u>Where they had not much earth: and forthwith they sprung up.</u>

The fact that scripture says that they sprung up suggests that he was saved and did persevere (bear fruit) ... for a short while. There are four sowers in this parable. The first sower was not saved hence you won't see any reference to his faith springing up. Scripture says that Satan came and stole the seed so that it couldn't become saving faith. (Luke 8:12.)

Then cometh the devil, and taketh away the word out of their hearts, lest they should believe and be saved.

The first sower was lost, the second and third sowers fell away (didn't persevere), the third sower was the only one that was faithful to the end.

Some may still disagree that the second and third sowers were saved. Well, then why does it say in Matthew 13:8 that some reaped thirtyfold, sixtyfold and a hundredfold? The doctrine of P.O.T.S. would only allow for the "hundredfold reaping" and besides why would lost or non-persevering Christians reap thirty and sixtyfold?

Obviously they were saved. The thirty and sixtyfold refer to rewards in heaven.

Do lost people get rewards in heaven?

Could a proponent of P.O.T.S. please explain this?

Their doctrine is twisted, senseless, ludicrous, manmade, anti-scriptural and prideful. The Calvinistic doctrine of P.O.T.S. is pure heresy! If you put faith in Christ for salvation, you are saved the very instant you do so. Nothing can change or reverse this. No persevering or non-persevering has anything you do with your salvific state. Works are the fruit of your salvation not the root of it.

The doctrine of P.O.T.S. suggests, insists, and demands that Christians must be faithful or remain in a state of faithfulness. But, it is true that God remains faithful even when we don't. 2 Timothy 2:13.

No human being is faithful all the time!

But God is.

Psalm 36:5 — *Thy mercy, O LORD, is in the heavens; and thy faithfulness reacheth unto the clouds.*

1 Corinthians 1:9 — *God is faithful, by whom ye were called unto the fellowship of his Son Jesus Christ our Lord.*

The gospel is faith alone in Christ. One simple act of faith. It is not continual faithfulness, which is what P.O.T.S. demand.

Scripture says:

Mark 11:22 — *And Jesus answering saith unto them, Have faith in God.*

Notice that he doesn't say: have <u>faithfulness</u> in God. I'm not discouraging faithfulness I'm just saying that what the law demands in terms of faithfulness is for the most part an unattainable pipedream.

Rejoice in the Lord always, pray without ceasing, go sin no more, in all thy way acknowledge him, love your enemies, be ye perfect, confess your faults one to another.

Yes, we are encouraged to do these things but does anyone you know rejoice in the Lord ALWAYS! Imagine someone praising God with every word he speaks, praying 24-7, never sinning in thought, dead, or word, acknowledging God in every instance, loving his enemies even when they severely wrong him, confessing every one of his faults to his fellow Christian nonstop, invariably.

That would be even an understated requirement for true faithfulness and nobody qualifies! Those who promote Lordship salvation and POTS are self-righteous hypocrites for even thinking that they are, will or must persevere to the end. Silly! We all sin, we all fall short and we all lack faith.

I tell people sometimes what I think true, unreserved faith is. It is going to the grocery store with a list of items, let's say ten dollars worth. You should pray fervently for God to miraculously put five dollars on the ground at the grocery store. Furthermore, you should only bring five dollars with you. Now, just trust that God will provide for you the other five dollars. You could come to the grocery store penniless to demonstrate extreme faith, but if you are not willing to have this kind of unreserved faith, then your faith is far from being faith<u>FULL</u>!

Here is a list of problems with P.O.T.S.

The thief on the cross.

How was he able to persevere?

Luke 23:42 — *And he said unto Jesus, Lord, remember me when thou comest into thy kingdom.*

What was Jesus' reply?

Was it ... persevere?

Was it ... do good works?

Was it ... be faithful.

No.

Luke 23:43 — *And Jesus said unto him, Verily I say unto thee, Today shalt thou be with me in paradise.*

Jesus refutes the doctrine of P.O.T.S.!

Some may say that the thief, had he the opportunity to come down off the cross would be under different orders. But this is just man babbling for the sake of argument and not Biblical.

Salvation is the same for everyone! Faith alone in Christ. Perseverance of the saints is a perversion of the gospel. If it is explained to someone before they are saved, they won't get saved, unless they are deceived into thinking that they can in their own flesh ... persevere. Such a mentality, according to the Bible, has not the humility to even see a need for salvation. We come to Christ: broken, sinful, helpless, bound by the flesh.

We don't come to Him with self-righteousness and no admission that we are helpless sinners.

Romans 5:7 — *For scarcely for a righteous man will one die: yet peradventure for a good man some would even dare to die.*

Rewards.

The doctrine of P.O.T.S. would not have much room for the doctrine of eternal rewards. Because if every believer perseveres then how are rewards meted out?

You persevered; you get a Cadillac.

You persevered; you get a Cadillac.

You really persevered; you get a Cadillac with shiny rims and a golden muffler.

Scripture makes it plain in 1 Corinthians 3:12 that there will be six types of works. Three good. Three bad.

Gold, silver, precious-stones, wood, hay, stubble.

If everyone persevered, then who will be representing the worthless hay, wood, and stubble?

The answer is, nobody.

What about Christians who die in a coma?

How can a comatose person persevere? Let me guess, when they are enduring a reverie, they must dream only wholesome thoughts. Nonsense. The contingencies, exigencies, pendencies, unpredictabilities, and imponderables of life can and do stymie the possibility of persevering.

P.O.T.S. is just not logical.

Perseverance of The Saints redefines love.

If someone had to persevere and some Calvinists will say that it automatically flows from saving faith, then how is love defined? You love God because you persevere. Well what about those that love God but don't persevere? Does that discount their love? No more than a divorcee divorcing their spouse. Love is not predicated by perseverance. Saying that love requires perseverance is bordering on terrorism. But what about the idea of perseverance naturally flowing from salvation? Once again, that is a rhetorical subtlety that really isn't any different than saying that salvation requires perseverance.

Imagine if someone thought that they had to persevere in a relationship in order to prove their love for their partner, wouldn't that seem a little fishy? Would it make you think that they didn't understand what true, natural love is? <u>Want to</u>, not <u>have to</u>. We should want to persevere, not think that we have to. The doctrine of P.O.T.S. implicitly suggests that we have to. How do I know this? Because they deem all non-perseverers as lost people.

So if you don't want to be considered lost according to their doctrine you <u>must</u> persevere! That reeks of being a demand. The doctrine of P.O.T.S. is more focused on man's love for God and not God's love for man. We should love God with all our hearts as scripture proclaims.

Mark 12:30 — *And thou shalt love the Lord thy God with all thy heart, and with all thy soul, and with all thy mind, and with all thy strength: this is the first commandment.*

We must always remember that God first loved us and His love for us is greater than our love for Him.

1 John 4:10 — *Herein is love, not that we loved God, but that he loved us, and sent his Son to be the propitiation for our sins.*

If P.O.T.S. were true then why on earth would anyone love God? If a god that demanded perseverance were the true God then how could anyone trust him? Especially when nobody knows if they even have the power to persevere in the future to come. I've known preachers that became full-bore alcoholics that cussed like sailors. I know all sorts of Christians that no longer walk in the faith. I would have to be ignorant and arrogant to just assume that they were all just never saved.

P.O.T.S. undermines God's keeping power and faithfulness.

John 6:37 — *All that the Father giveth me shall come to me; and him that cometh to me I will in no wise cast out.*

It doesn't say that those who don't persevere will be cast out.

It says that all that the father gives me shall come to me. Coming to me by simple faith in Christ is the qualifier for being not cast out—not perseverance!

The proponents of P.O.T.S. are confused. Some say that their doctrine just means staying faithful to the end despite periodic sins. Some try to redefine faith as not practicing or living in sin. But the Bible contains both those who fell away from the faith and those who habitually sinned.

Samson.

Judges 16:1 — *Then went Samson to Gaza, and saw there an harlot, and went in unto her.*

Samson ended his life in adultery and suicide, yet he was still saved as it is recorded in Hebrews 11:32.

What about dying in persistent sin.

Hebrews 11:31 — *By faith the <u>harlot</u> Rahab perished not with them that believed not, when she had received the spies with peace.*

This clearly states that Rahab was saved. In the Old Testament Rahab was consistently called a harlot—that was her profession. So, clearly she lived in this sin thoroughpaced.

Psalm 89:29-33 — *His seed also will I make to endure for ever, and his throne as the days of heaven. If his children <u>forsake my law</u>, and <u>walk not in my judgments</u>; If they <u>break my statutes</u>, and <u>keep not my commandments</u>; Then will I visit their transgression with the rod, and their iniquity with stripes. Nevertheless my lovingkindness will I not utterly take from him, nor suffer my faithfulness to fail.*

Forsaking my law, walking not in judgments, breaking statutes, keeping not my commandments. This doesn't sound like perseverance; yet God promises that his faithfulness will not fail nor will his covenant be broken.

Assurance of salvation.

P.O.T.S. makes assurance of salvation a present-tense uncertainty.

P.O.T.S. makes assurance of salvation a postmortem discovery. If you don't know that you will persevere then you can't know that you are saved even now. You may end up in hell thinking to yourself, I didn't lose my salvation; I just never had it in the first place. Scripture is clear that you can know you have salvation in this lifetime (1 John 5:13, 20, Romans 4:16, John 6:69).

Besides what would motivate us to do good deeds and live after the spirit if we had no assurance of salvation? The doctrine of P.O.T.S. changes our reason for serving God. They serve God not out of love but out of the fear of hell.

It's a terrible doctrine.

It causes non-perseverers to doubt their salvation and ultimately give up on Christianity!

Conclusion.

The doctrine of Perseverance of the Saints does many negative things. It distorts scriptures, changes the gospel, and demands something from man that man doesn't have the aptitude to live up to. It engenders pride, self-righteousness and arrogance in its espousers.

Think about it.

If someone says and thinks that they are persevering, they are not focused on what Christ has done for them at Calvary, they are more focused on their own filthy, raggedy works. Sick! They are accusing non-perseverers as being unworthy of salvation—that's judgmental and pious!

The P.O.T.S. is simply a doctrine of Satan. We should deny Calvinism in all its forms!

Free grace is the only biblical doctrine when it comes to the true gospel.

John 3:16 is the gospel in a nutshell. It's the gospel in twenty-five words (KJV) and it clearly refutes P.O.T.S.

It doesn't say:

John 3:16 — *For God so loved the world, that he gave his only begotten Son, that whosoever believeth <u>and persevereth</u> in him should not perish, but have everlasting life.*

The doctrine of P.O.T.S. is a demanding doctrine and if God demanded anything from us it would be sinless perfection. That is, by the way, imputed to us through faith in Christ. So if you take P.O.T.S. to its logical conclusion you are demanding sinless perfection whether you realize it or not. John 3:16 doesn't say anything about perseverance. It simply says we must believe.

John 3:16 — *For God so loved the world, that he gave his only begotten Son, that whosoever <u>BELIEVETH</u> in him should not perish, but have everlasting life.*

Believe ... not persevere.
Faith Alone. THE WAY TO CHRIST.

Chapter 12

Security in the Old Testament

Eternal security is a biblical fact! There's no honest debate about the subject, but some theologians believed that the OT believers were not secure. I hope to explain how and why that is wrong. Hebrews 13:8.

When I first wrote this manuscript, I could have entitled it: The Goodness Of Christ or Christ Will Never Leave You. I could've entitled it anything. Eternal security is what makes Christianity distinct from other religions. It's what makes the gospel good news (glad tidings, Luke 1:19.) If we weren't secure in Christ, this book would be pointless, but so would life and our Christian walk!

The reason for this subset is to show you that security is consistent in the Bible and it can be found in the Old Testament as well as the New Testament.

I've devoted this subset in declaring the security we have in Christ based on the Old Testament promises.

First of all David the Psalmist had full security in God, security that God would not fail him and that salvation was certain. Could he have used such language had he felt otherwise?

O give thanks unto the LORD; for he is good; for his mercy endureth for ever.

O LORD, there is none like thee, neither is there any God beside thee, according to all that we have heard with our ears. (Chronicles 16:34, 17:20).

He knew that salvation wasn't something that constantly hung in the balance like an active pendulum. Salvation wasn't a fickle or fluctuant thing. The Bible uses pretty strong language when it describes salvation.

1 Chronicles 16:17 — *And hath confirmed the same to Jacob for a law, and to Israel for an everlasting covenant.*

Sounds pretty secure.

125:2.

As the mountains are round about Jerusalem, so the LORD is round about his people from henceforth even for ever.

Psalm 37:28-29 — *For the LORD loveth judgment, and forsaketh not his saints; they are preserved for ever: but the seed of the wicked shall be cut off. The righteous shall inherit the land, and dwell therein for ever.*

These verses in the Old Testament prove that we are perfectly secure in Christ.

The doctrine of eternal security is essential to understanding everything else about the Bible. Here are some more OT verses that prove that we are secure in Christ.

Psalm 37:23-24 — *The steps of a good man are ordered by the LORD: and he delighteth in his way. Though he fall, he shall not be utterly cast down: for the LORD upholdeth him with his hand.*

I used the forthcoming verses in my last subset to disprove the doctrine of perseverance of the saints and my emphasis was on Israel and their lack of obedience. Look at these verses again with the emphasis this time on God's promises.

Psalms 89:29-34 — *His seed also will I make to endure for ever, and his throne as the days of heaven. If his children forsake my law, and walk not in my judgments; If they break my statutes, and keep not my commandments; Then will I visit their transgression with the rod, and their iniquity with stripes. Nevertheless* <u>*my loving kindness will I not utterly take from him*</u>, *nor suffer my* <u>*faithfulness to fail*</u>. *My covenant will* <u>*I not break*</u>, *nor alter the thing that is gone out of my lips. Once have I sworn by my holiness that I will not lie unto David.*

The Old Testament is replete with verses on security.

Genesis 17:7 — *And I will establish my covenant between me and thee and thy seed after thee in their generations for an everlasting covenant, to be a God unto thee, and to thy seed after thee.*

Psalm 41:13 — *Blessed be the LORD God of Israel from everlasting, and to everlasting. Amen, and Amen.*

Isaiah 45:17 — *But Israel shall be saved in the LORD with an everlasting salvation: ye shall not be ashamed nor confounded world without end.*

There are some verses in both the OT and NT that when the word 'salvation' or *teshuah,* is used are not referring to eternal salvation. *Teshuah* in Hebrew refers to just physical deliverance or being rescued from dire circumstances, but the Isaiah 45:17 reference is obviously about eternal salvation for it clearly says everlasting salvation. This is a promise of security. Temporal salvation is obviously not eternal. Eternal salvation obviously is!

Ezekiel 16:60 — *Nevertheless I will remember my covenant with thee in the days of thy youth, and I will establish unto thee an everlasting covenant.*

Daniel 9:24 — *Seventy weeks are determined upon thy people and upon thy holy city, to finish the transgression, and to make an end of sins, and to make reconciliation for iniquity, and to bring in everlasting righteousness, and to seal up the vision and prophecy, and to anoint the most Holy.*

Faith Alone. THE WAY TO CHRIST.

Chapter 13

In Christ

The Christian life is shallow and unanimated until we realize the biblical truth of our position in Christ. Scripture says that we are baptized in Christ.

Romans 6:3 — *Know ye not, that so many of us as were baptized into Jesus Christ were baptized into his death?*

This verse confirms the reality of our security in Christ. Baptized into Christ Jesus—now! Baptized into His death—eternity!

Baptizo in Greek denotes being identified with Christ by association. Nothing can alter this.

The idea of undoing any of these promises would require someone to be unbaptized which just doesn't make any logical sense. Our position in Christ is like a lifetime membership at the YMCA. We may only attend for a few months periodically, but that doesn't mean that after three decades of nonattendance and then later we decide to return, that our membership has expired. No. It is a lifetime membership. Nothing can change that. Same with our position in Christ.

1 Corinthians 15:22 — *For as in Adam all die, even so in Christ shall all be made alive.*

"In" in the Greek is *en*, which means 'fixed' or a fixed position. When something is fixed in place you can be certain that nothing can alter it.

Romans 16:7 — *Salute Andronicus and Junia, my kinsmen, and my fellow-prisoners, who are of note among the apostles, who also were in Christ before me.*

Romans 8:1 — *There is therefore now no condemnation to them which are in Christ Jesus, who walk not after the flesh, but after the Spirit.*

It is God that establishes us into Christ.

2 Corinthians 1:21 — *Now he which stablisheth us with you in Christ, and hath anointed us, is God.*

It is important to understand this positional reality of our salvation. So many people, especially opponents of Free Grace put an emphasis on how we live, how we are walking with Christ, or growing spiritually and these are important components of sanctification, not justification, but the salient truth is that if we are born-again Christians through faith in Christ, we are in Him. Like marbles in a jar hermetically sealed and awaiting heaven.

Scripture doesn't say that we are next to Christ, near Christ, partnered with Christ or holding Christ's hand. Opponents of Free Grace would purport such scenarios and the fringe of such hypotheses would always give the Christian little to no assurance of salvation unless those near, next to, partnered with or holding Christ's hand stayed faithful and obedient. But being in Christ secures us so durably that nothing we do, good or bad, can change the fact that we belong to Christ and are totally saved.

I used the analogy of marbles in a jar. The jar is Christ and He is indestructible. No matter what the marbles do whilst in the jar, no matter how turbulent or splenetic they might become therein, no amount of implosive combustion can break the jar!

2 Corinthians 5:17 — *Therefore if any man be in Christ, he is a new creature: old things are passed away; behold, all things are become new.*

When this says old things are passed away; it isn't saying that the old sins the believer used to commit are no more. We both know that Christians still wrestle with the same sins of his past by and by. The only difference between Christians and non-Christians is that the Christian possesses the Holy Spirit, prayer and scripture to help them in their battle against sin. When scripture says "old things" it is referring to the old nature passing away positionally, not experientially. "Old things" in Greek is *Archaios*, which means 'origin.' Our origin, hamartiologically speaking, is Adam and his sin nature.

Now, we both know that our sin nature hasn't passed away in its experience. If it had then there'd be sinless-little-Christs inhabiting the earth instead of heaven, which makes no sense. No sinless person except Christ has any business dwelling on the earth and likewise, no sinful person has any business being in heaven without his/her glorified body.

When scripture says that old things are passed away, it is talking about our position in which we stand before God now and on judgment day.

This has nothing to do with our current sinfulness and carnal nature that still leave us pitiably struggling. Some people have said, with vagueness, that once you are saved, at least part of your old nature is gone and that is why we don't sin as much as the non-believer. This is the error of eradicationism (the idea that your sin nature is progressively eradicated in time) Such a statement fails to understand the Holy Spirit's role in the spiritual life and also the fact that such an attitude leaves us self-righteous and ignorant about seemingly smaller sins which paradoxically become larger sins, i.e., pride, arrogance, prejudice.

Once we understand our position in Christ—our mindset about sin, assurance, grace and judgment all change.

Galatians 3:28 — *There is neither Jew nor Greek, there is neither bond nor free, there is neither male nor female: for ye are all one <u>in Christ</u> Jesus.*

Philippians 4:21 — *Salute every saint <u>in Christ</u> Jesus. The brethren which are with me greet you.*

****

Being in Christ covers several areas of salvation, sin, assurance, grace and judgment.

Sin. No matter what kind, how many or how much a Christian engages in it, he is still <u>in Christ</u>. Sin is no longer an issue because it was condemned in Christ's flesh. (Romans 8:3) (Romans 8:1.)

Assurance. We have full assurance of heaven because we are <u>in Christ</u>. (Isaiah 32:17.)

Grace. We have a standing in grace that can never be altered to those who are in Christ. (1 Peter 5:12.)

Judgment. We no longer have to be worried about a judicial, penal judgment because we are in Christ. Yet, we will be judged paternally, (lovingly) for our works, good or bad. (2 Corinthians 5:10.)

Although we are encouraged to do good works, (Ephesians 2:10), our works have nothing to do with our position in Christ. Our position in Christ is contingent only upon faith.

Ephesians 1:19-20 — *And what is the exceeding greatness of his power to us-ward who believe, according to the working of his mighty power, Which he wrought in Christ, when he raised him from the dead, and set him at his own right hand in the heavenly places.*

Verse 19 talks about believing and verse 20 explains our position. God has wrought us positionally in Christ. This is a supernatural work that man cannot modify or rework in anyway. The Bible is replete with verses on this subject.

Galatians 6:15 — *For in Christ Jesus neither circumcision availeth any thing, nor uncircumcision, but a new creature.*

In the Greek: uncircumcision, *Akrobustia* denotes a gentile or unregenerate person. And Circumcision, *Peritome*, represents someone with religious rites. But this was the case only according to the law. Since Christians are not under the law (any of the laws), neither circumcision nor uncircumcision matter. (Romans 6:14).

You could translate this verse to say this.

Galatians 6:15 — *For in Christ Jesus neither circumcision (good deeds) availeth any thing, nor uncircumcision (bad deeds), but a new creature.*

Even carnal Christians are <u>in Christ.</u>

1 Corinthians 3:3 — *For ye are yet carnal: for whereas there is among you envying, and strife, and divisions, are ye not carnal, and walk as men?*

Yeah, but how do we know that this is being addressed to true Christians? Well Paul's letter to the church of Corinth wasn't to unbelievers. None of his epistles were. Back up to chapter 1 verse: 30, Paul addresses them as those <u>in Christ</u>. He also calls them brethren in many Corinthian passages. (1:1, 2:1, 3:1. 10:1, 15:1.)

1 Corinthians 1:30 — *But of him are ye <u>in Christ Jesus</u>, who of God is made unto us wisdom, and righteousness, and sanctification, and redemption.*

It is our position in Christ that matters and all believers have this permanent, unshakable, irrevocable, impeccable standing with their Saviour that nothing can change, cancel, undo or nullify. (Romans 8:38-39.)

1 Corinthians1 5:22 — *For as in Adam all die, even so in Christ shall all be made alive.*

2 Corinthians 1:21 — *Now he which stablisheth us with you in Christ, and hath anointed us, is God.*

2 Corinthians 5:17 — *Therefore if any man be in Christ, he is a new creature: old things are passed away; behold, all things are become new.*

Galatians 1:22 — *And was unknown by face unto the churches of Judaea which were in Christ.*

Even entire churches were positionally in Christ.

Galatians 3:28 — *There is neither Jew nor Greek, there is neither bond nor free, there is neither male nor female: for ye are all one in Christ Jesus.*

What this is saying is that it doesn't matter who you are or what type of person you were, if you are a believer you are in Christ.

Ephesians 1:10 — *That in the dispensation of the fulness of times he might gather together in one all things in Christ, both which are in heaven, and which are on earth; even in him.*

Being in Christ is good news. But how do we know if our position promises us heaven. Take a look at these verses.

Ephesians 2:5-6 — *Even when we were dead in sins, hath quickened us together with Christ, (by grace ye are saved;)*

— And hath raised us up together, and made us sit together in heavenly places in Christ Jesus.

God quickens and even raises us to heaven. This position, "In Christ" is a reality to every believer. Not only are we in Christ, but the Bible submits that Christ is in us as well.

Colossians 1:27 — *To whom God would make known what is the riches of the glory of this mystery among the Gentiles; which is Christ <u>in you</u>, the hope of glory.*

Here are some more scriptures that explain our position in Christ versus our experience.

Children of light

The Bible describes Christians as being children of light or children of the day.

In 1 Thessalonians 5, Paul is writing to Christians and in the first verse Paul explains that they were believers that didn't even need to know what he was about to preach in terms of their salvation. He is explaining their position in Christ versus their experience.

1 — But of the times and the seasons, brethren, ye have no need that I write unto you.

2 — For yourselves know perfectly that the day of the Lord so cometh as a thief in the night.

In this verse he is reminded them of the rapture. Thief in the night is not to denote a negative act, only and act unforeseen.

3 — For when they shall say, Peace and safety; then sudden destruction cometh upon them, as travail upon a woman with child; and they shall not escape.

4 — But ye, brethren, are not in darkness, that that day should overtake you as a thief.

When he says that they are not in darkness he means positionally, not experientially. A person's lifestyle is not in question here.

5 — Ye are all the children of light, and the children of the day: we are not of the night, nor of darkness.

He now explains that they are children of light (positionally) children of light or of the day states the believer's position in Christ. It has nothing to do with how they are living because in the next verse he is exhorting them to live soberly.

6 — Therefore let us not sleep, as do others; but let us watch and be sober.

7 — For they that sleep sleep in the night; and they that be drunken are drunken in the night.

8 — But let us, who are of the day, (positionally) be sober, putting on the breastplate of faith and love; and for an helmet, the hope of salvation.

Be sober, put on faith, love and hope are exhortations that pertain to our experience. They have nothing to do with our position (children of the day or light), which can't be changed.

9 — For God hath not appointed us to wrath, but to obtain salvation by our Lord Jesus Christ,

10 — Who died for us, that, whether we wake (spiritual experience) or sleep, (carnal experience) we should live together with him.

The importance of understating this positional truth is so that we will be more motivated to allow our Christian experience to align with our declared position.

Faith alone. THE WAY TO CHRIST.

Chapter 14

East to West

It is a geographical impossibility to travel from an eastern apical point to a western apical point. We can get from south to north—and proof of this is the North Pole and the South Pole. Man is at the nadir of the south and God is at the vertex of the north. Man can get to God only through the cross. (Faith in Jesus.) But if God dwelt in the east and man in the west, no nexus could be made because horizontal space is infinitely separated.

It would defy the law of gravity to get from an eastern apex to a western apex. It's just not scientifically or geographically possible.

Psalm 103:12 says that: *As far as the east is from the west, so far hath he removed our transgressions from us.*

'Removed' in the Greek is *Rachaq*. This means: "to place at a distance." And scripture confirms that the distance is from east to west—which is the most unbridgeable two distances in the universe. The aphelion (low-point) to apogee (high-point) nexus works only vertically because the earth and the firmament are two real places.

If God has removed our sins or placed them at a distance that is from east to west, then there is no way He can ever see our sins again. Imagine Him staring into the Far East; our sins are directly behind the back of his head in the Far West. Even if He were to turn 180 degrees, the sins would then go to the other polar apical distance. From east to west, from west to east.

Compare this verse to:

Isaiah 38:17 — *Behold, for peace I had great bitterness: but thou hast in love to my soul delivered it from the pit of corruption: for thou hast cast all my sins <u>behind thy back</u>.*

Behind my back is "east to west" in comparison.

Salvation can't be lost in any capacity. Because if it could then God would have to impute sin back to man. A sin that has been removed to such a magnitude would have to be reinstituted. This is not possible!

Science and geography have proven that salvation cannot be lost in any capacity. And furthermore that free grace theology is the only way that such perfect unity between man and God is possible.

Faith Alone. THE WAY TO CHRIST.

Chapter 15

Faith Alone Promises Us Eternal Life!

According to history, the term: "Sola Fide" has only been around in theological circles since 1517, but the concept found in the Bible dates back to as early as Genesis.

This is a key Sola Fide verse, and I have, by now, in all my theological writings, used it tautologically.

Genesis 15:6 — *And he believed in the LORD; and he counted it to him for righteousness.*

Abram was justified by faith alone while he was yet uncircumcised. He was so rich in good works but was not justified by them. Same with anybody else. We are justified by faith alone. This is the earliest account of evidence for Sola Fide.

This doctrine not only started out in Genesis, but is still good for its' offer today and it absolutely promises salvation!

Hebrews 6:12 — *That ye be not slothful, but followers of them who through faith and patience inherit the promises.*

The word "promise", according to the dictionary, means:

"An expression of assurance on which expectation is to be based."

God cannot break a promise.

Hebrews 6:18 — *That by two immutable things, in which it was impossible for God to lie (or break a promise), we might have a strong consolation, who have fled for refuge to lay hold upon the hope set before us.*

Emphasis mine.

Scriptures buttress the fact that God promises us salvation through Sola Fide.

Acts 2:39 — *For the <u>promise</u> is unto you, and to your children, and to all that are afar off, even as many as the LORD our God shall call.*

Romans 4:16 — *Therefore it is of faith, that it might be by grace; to the end the <u>promise</u> might be sure to all the seed; not to that only which is of the law, but to that also which is of the faith of Abraham; who is the father of us all.*

Romans 4:13 — *For the <u>promise</u>, that he should be the heir of the world, was not to Abraham, or to his seed, through the law, but through the righteousness of faith.*

Some skeptics might say that this promise was the inheritance of the world, and not heaven, but read the following verses.

1 Timothy 4:8 — *For bodily exercise profiteth little: but godliness is profitable unto all things, having* **promise** *of the life that now is, and of that which <u>is to come</u>.*

"Is to come" is clearly talking about the afterlife in heaven.

2 Peter 3:13 — *Nevertheless we, according to his* **promise**, *look for <u>new heavens</u> and a new earth, wherein dwelleth righteousness.*

"New heavens" is talking about the afterlife.

1 John 2:25 — *And this is the promise that he hath* **promised** *us, even <u>eternal life</u>.*

Titus 1:2 — *In hope of eternal life, which God, that cannot lie,* **promised** *before the world began.*

Not only was it promised; it was promised before the world began which renders such a promise subject to no influential force for there was nothing that could negate such a promise that came about before THE WORLD BEGAN!

And lastly, here's a three-point hitter for Sola Fide.

Ephesians 1:13 — *In whom ye also trusted, after that ye heard the word of truth, the gospel of your <u>salvation</u>: in whom also after that ye <u>believed</u>, ye were sealed with that Holy Spirit of <u>promise</u>.*

Sola Fide promises salvation and this irrefutable verse is all one needs to prove it!

If Sola Fide weren't true then the original writers of these verses have some explaining to do. Why would God, who cannot lie and break a promise, have inseminated His word with such wonderful promises? That's exactly what the opponents of Sola Fide have to stand on in the constitution of their contemptible doctrine, ... broken promises!

Another thing that free grace theology offers is positivism. Below is an extraction from my manuscript: Free Not Cheap. A list written out paragraphically of many positive features of free grace theology.

Salvation. Grace. Joy. Peace. Justification. Redemption. Mercy. Truth. Remission of sin. Progressive sanctification. Eternal security. Spiritual adoption. Sonship. Heirship to the Kingdom. Eternity. God is good.

Below is a list of God-facets where two negative invaders are present. The reason I'm pointing this out is because if faith is not alone or if grace is not totally free then you would have myriad anti-grace invaders.

The invaders are:

"Works" and "losing salvation."

Notice that a little leaven has leavened the whole lump.

Salvation. <u>Works</u>. Joy. Peace. Justification. Redemption. Mercy. Truth. Remission of sin. Progressive sanctification. <u>Losing salvation</u>. Spiritual adoption. Sonship. Heirship to the kingdom. Eternity. God is good.

If "works" or "losing salvation" were true, then the promise of eternal life would be impeded and the whole lump would now poisonously appear as...

Conditional Salvation. <u>Works.</u> Joylessness. No Peace. No Justification. Irrevocable Redemption. Comeuppance. Uncertainty. Limited atonement of sin. Necessary sanctification. <u>Losing salvation.</u> Impersonal Adoption. Conditional Sonship. Insecure heirship to the Kingdom. Temporality. Man must be good. Condemnation.

What good would God's promise of eternal life be if salvation were not by faith alone?

Chapter 16

Five Characteristics of a Disciple

Keep in mind that a disciple is not necessarily a Christian and a Christian is not necessarily a disciple. A disciple is someone who is living after the spirit. Carnal Christians, who do exist, 1 Corinthians 3:1-4, are not active disciples. Disciples have to be trained (John 4:1). This subset is to encourage us to be disciples.

BCS-*best case scenario.*

WCS-*worse case scenario.*

Hunger for God.

Matthew 4:4.

Craving to know God, the things of God, spiritual things, truth, Godly wisdom.

BCS-craving for meat, studying doctrine. Having a deep yearning for Biblical truth.

WCS-craving milk, asking a few questions about God.

Bible reading.

Acts 17:11.

Reading, studying, daily Bible time.

BCS-studying the Bible avidly, for long hours, note taking, and concordance studies.

WCS-reluctantly spending minimal time in Bible. Few verses a day.

Prayer life.

1 Thessalonians 5:19.

Supplications, praises, talking to God.

BCS-long, request-driven, prayer whilst quoting scriptures. Contemplative prayers.

WCS-pithy before meal prayers (few seconds a day).

Or before bed.

Church.

Matthew 16:18.

Gathering together with other believers. Fellowship.

BCS-church twice or three times a week, church programs, home Bible studies.

WCS-Once-a-week Sunday morning church.

Confession of sins.

1 John 1:9.

Openly admit to God you sin, when you sin, daily.

BCS-contritely admit you have sinned, forgive yourself and move on into spirituality.

WCS-confess every once and a while without remorse or repentance.

****

Now what if not all or none of these characteristics are there?

Well, that means that a child of God of this type is miserable.

Romans 6:1, 15. Hebrews 12:11.

Other characteristics such as: downloading sermons, fasting, memorizing scriptures, meditative prayers, fighting off or abstaining from sin, writing Christian books, poetry, music, giving to the needy, etc, etc are all symptomatic of discipleship not salvation. The five characteristics of a Christian should eventually manifest themselves in the life of the growing believer. If not, misery caused by chastisement must be there. The idea of a Christian that is manifesting NONE of the following characteristics and yet perfectly happy and content and without chastisement is foreign to scriptures for even the carnal church of Corinth was chastised.

This is not to discourage. Don't read this and say: man, my spiritual walk is not that good. I don't pray (enough). I don't read my Bible (enough). I don't go to church (enough), I don't confess my sins (enough), I don't hunger for the things of God (enough).

Well then start ...

Praying (more).

Reading the Bible (more).

Confessing your sins (more).

Going to church (more).

Get hungry for the things of God (more).

Get encouraged! Not discouraged.

But what about grace?

Am I saying that people have to do these things in order to be saved? No. Grace is totally free. I'm not even suggesting that these things will flow from us because of grace. I'm saying that it is highly unlikely that a true born-again Christian will not experience some of these characteristics at least from time to time. It's just natural to experience these fruits when the real Holy Spirit indwelling takes place. I don't think this is too harsh—although some may disagree.

The likelihood of a true Christian not being marked by any of these characteristics without chastisement would be like me tossing fifty coins into the air and each landing on heads. It's possible but highly unlikely!

We are secure in Christ. I put this subset first to eradicate any charges of lawlessness, antinomianism or grace-abuse that some of the works-heretics may throw at me. Security is why we should be diligent in our Christian walk.

Man cannot live by bread alone but by every word that proceedeth out of the mouth of God.

Chapter 17

Defending Free Grace

Is free grace for itching ears?

2 Timothy 4:3 — *For the time will come when they will not endure sound doctrine; but after their own lusts shall they heap to themselves teachers, having itching ears.*

Some of the opponents of free grace accuse free gracers of giving a message that is simply scratching the itching ears of its' listeners. People just want to hear this. You are saved by grace and then you can go out and sin all you want and still get to heaven. That's just what sinners want to hear. To their own chagrin, this message is true—however incomplete.

The gospel par excellence is just that but should be explained better. Christ died for all your sins. Once you accept His free gift by faith, you will go to heaven no matter what you do. Anything less than this is a works salvation heresy.

If free grace scratches itching ears then works-salvation just irritates the itch!

If works were part of salvation, then by implication you are saying that man owes God. But that's not where it stops. If God required man to do good works; then God therefore owes man. The essence of this false gospel from every angle would be nothing shy of quid pro quo. You might as well just auction off grace to the highest bidder.

The good news of the gospel should do more than just tickle your ears; it should sooth the deepest ache in the inmost depth of your soul. The ear-tickling accusation is just a worthless strawman. Any message that opposes free grace is predicated by negativism. What 2 Timothy is talking about has nothing to do with free grace. It has to do with abusing grace. The free grace message—as maligned by the workists—does not give man a license to sin, this too is a farcical strawman. You won't read in this book or by any of the honorable free grace writers that I know of that it is okay to sin or that sin has no consequences. You might read that you can go on sinning and still get to heaven, which is true by the way. If not, heaven would be dull, peopleless and vacuous. Or you may read that you shouldn't sin but you are going to because of your sin-nature!

But you will not read, not from this book anyway, that sin pays. Nor will you read that sin has no temporary consequences. In my previous manuscript: Sola Fide, I wrote about what happens to a Christian who keeps on sinning. I will sum it up here.

If we keep on sinning...

1. We temporarily break fellowship with God. (Psalm 51:12.)

2. We become ashamed. (Genesis 3:10.)

3. We get chastised. (Hebrews 12:8.)

4. We lose rewards in heaven. (1 Corinthians 3:15.)

5. We grieve the Holy Spirit. (Ephesians 4:30.)

6. We become grieved ourselves. (Hebrews 12:11.)

7. We expedite physical death. (1 Corinthians 5:5.)

8. We ruin our Christian witness. (1 John 3:8.)

9. We lose subjective assurance of salvation. (2 Peter 1:10.)

10. We necessitate confession. (1 John 1:9.)

This doesn't sound like a message that tickles ears, does it? The erroneous accusations that free grace is just "sweet talk" or "ear-tickling" would have to exclude any of these biblical consequences to sin. For me to tickle ears, I would have to say that you could keep on sinning and nothing consequential will happen. God won't chastise you. In fact, he rewards bad behavior. But this is not biblical and I'm not saying this.

The haters of free grace try to accuse us of implicitly saying this. Because, they feel, if God doesn't damn the saved sinner to hell, they think that nothing else will happen to that sinner. Obviously, they only have two polar extremes in mind. Heaven or hell. If you're good you go to heaven and if you're bad you go to hell. This is essentially their theology, which is totally secularistic. They have eliminated any gray area where existential discipline is executed and eternal rewards are earned or lost.

The opponents of free grace (heretics), have eliminated the following:

Possibilities of rewards. (They feel that sin results in damnation, so where is the need for rewards?)

A need for confession. (They feel that sinning cancels salvation, so where is the need to confess?)

Chastisement. (They feel that God damns the saved sinner so where is the need for chastisement?)

Grace. (They feel that if you keep on sinning you aren't saved. This knows nothing of grace!)

Forgiveness. (They feel that if you keep sinning, you're damned. Where's the forgiveness?)

Forensic justification. (They feel that if you keep on sinning, you aren't justified. So who can be justified?)

Spiritual growth. (They feel that if you keep on sinning then you don't have salvation. So obviously they expect all Christians upon conversion to be spiritually mature. How ridiculous?)

Carnal Christianity. (They feel that there's no such thing as a carnal Christian. Then why did Paul call some of his followers carnal?)

Hope for the sinner. (They condemn saved sinners, but God doesn't. (Romans 4:6-8, v 8:1)

Plenary atonement. (They maintain that works are necessary for atonement. So why don't they circumcise themselves then?)

The proper motivation to serve God. (They serve God only from fear of hell. Which is twisted, morbid and lacking of real appreciatory love.)

The doctrine of original sin. (They say that you are required to stop sinning, then couldn't Adam have done something to not transmit his genetic sin nature to the world?)

Every branch the workist has eliminated from the theological tree of Biblical truth is integral to free grace. The opponents of free grace offer nothing but a fraudulent scam that sends them to hell. And they have the audacity to say that I'm tickling ears. If I'm tickling them, it is only because their noxious (conditional salvation) travesty is sprinkling on the irritating itch-powder.

Romans 3:24 — *Being justified freely by his grace through the redemption that is in Christ Jesus.*

What about those people who try to use the book of James to say that the Bible teaches faith plus works? Or faith without works is dead faith, which by intimation they mean not faith at all. Well you should ask them: is a car without gas or motor fuel not a car?

So many people say that dead faith is not faith at all. This is heresy! Is a car without gas not a car? No. It's a car that can't be driven; but it's still a car.

James 2:20 — *But wilt thou know, O vain man, that faith without works is dead?*

James 2:26 — *For as the body without the spirit is dead, so faith without works is dead also.*

Faith needs no work. So what do these scriptures mean?

It means that faith, which you once had for salvation is now dead or inactive. What should we do? The synergists or Lordship Salvationists would say that we need to have true, saving faith in Christ, (whatever that means.) Dead faith does not mean no-faith; it simply means that their faith isn't doing anything. It's like a car without gas. You don't need to chunk the car and get a new one; you just need to put some gas in it. If you have dead faith, your faith needs to be revitalized—plain and simple. It's a tragedy how these scriptures have been wrangled out of context to promote Lordship Salvation. In my Sola Fide manuscript I wrote an excerpt explaining this.

"James chapter 2 seems to be describing the type of faith that I am promoting—faith that proves itself by works. That is not what I'm talking about. Faith must have an object. The object is Christ. The finished work on the cross.

James 2:24 — *Ye see then how that by works a man is justified, and not by faith only.*

First of all, this justification is not salvific justification. It is justification before man. Man justifies on the basis of what he empirically sees. Faith, according to the principal of ding-an-sich, is invisible. Man justifies by what he sees, namely: works.

Romans 3:20 — *Therefore by the deeds of the law there shall no flesh be justified in his sight: for by the law is the knowledge of sin.*

Key words: no flesh shall be justified in his (God's) sight.

Romans 4:2 — *For if Abraham were justified by works, he hath whereof to glory; but not before God.*

Glory means, "boast" or "brag."

If Abraham is not boasting before God, he is boasting before man hence seeking man's justification for his good works.

It is God who justifies.

Romans 8:33 — *Who shall lay any thing to the charge of God's elect? It is God that justifieth."*

People with dead faith aren't lost; they are just inert Christians. Here's a biblical example of someone with dead faith.

James 2:16-17 — *And one of you say unto them, Depart in peace, be ye warmed and filled; notwithstanding ye give them not those things which are needful to the body; what doth it profit? Even so faith, if it hath not works, is dead, being alone.*

If dead faith meant lost then wouldn't this mean that every stingy, tightfisted person who is not willing to give a derelict some pocket-change was lost. If that's the case then no one is going to heaven! Dead faith would be that which is characteristic of a backslider.

Backsliders are recidivated babes in Christ. We need to re-baby-feed them.

Hebrews 5:13-14.

13—For every one that useth milk is unskilful in the word of righteousness: for he is a babe.

Christians with proactive, alive, and burgeoning faith need meat. The meat of scripture is doctrine and exegesis. The milk is simply daily readings of practical scriptures.

14—But strong meat belongeth to them that are of full age, even those who by reason of use have their senses exercised to discern both good and evil.

How are we to feed babes in Christ?

Little by little.

I think it isn't healthy to try to cram too much biblical food into someone who isn't spiritual.

Scripture uses the analogy of "milk" and "meat."

Isaiah 28:10 — *For precept must be upon precept, precept upon precept; line upon line, line upon line; here a little, and there a little.*

How do I know this is referring to the word of God analogous to spiritual food?

Look at verse 9.

Whom shall he teach knowledge? and whom shall he make to understand doctrine? them that are weaned from the milk, and drawn from the breasts.

Bible reading is assimilated to breastfeeding.

Verse thirteen clarifies this. Line upon line, precept upon precept, here a little there a little.

Isaiah 28:13.

But the word of the LORD was unto them precept upon precept, precept upon precept; line upon line, line upon line; here a little, and there a little; that they might go, and fall backward, and be broken, and snared, and taken.

This is the solution for dead faith. Sanctification.

James 2 is simply instructing us to not be stagnant in our faith. It doesn't mean we never had real faith despite what the opponents of free grace posit.

Faith Alone is the way to Christ.

Chapter 18

READ YOUR BIBLE!

Faith needs no work and we as Christians don't have to nor can we earn eternal life by works for it is all of grace. It does behoove us to grow spiritually. So many Christians are confused as to how. They think that spirituality is simply to stop sinning. They are dead wrong, deceived and calling God a liar, (1 John 1:10) for even the greatest saint still sins. (Ecclesiastes 7:20) If a person thinks that they don't sin, they are carnal, plain and simple.

The only way to not sin would be to lock yourself in a straight-jacket, get sedated by Demerol—don't enjoy the sedation—squirm and writhe around in the enclosing confines of a rubber-room with the lights out. This would be the closest a person could come to not sinning, but it would still be a sin for some greater deed could have supplanted this madness.

Those who claim to not sin have to explain how they get through the day without renaming their sins. Spiritual growth starts with doing spiritual things. Like prayer, fasting, soul-winning, giving to the needy, attending church and most importantly Bible reading!

Read your Bibles...

****

Deuteronomy 17:19 — *And it shall be with him, and he shall read therein all the days of his life: that he may learn to fear the LORD his God, to keep all the words of this law and these statutes, to do them.*

Joshua 8:34 — *And afterward he read all the words of the law, the blessings and cursings, according to all that is written in the book of the law.*

Matthew 22:29 — *Jesus answered and said unto them, Ye do err, not knowing the scriptures, nor the power of God.*

John 5:39 — *Search the scriptures; for in them ye think ye have eternal life: and they are they which testify of me.*

Acts 17:11 — *These were more noble than those in Thessalonica, in that they received the word with all readiness of mind, and searched the scriptures daily, whether those things were so.*

Luke 4:4 — *And Jesus answered him, saying, It is written, That man shall not live by bread alone, but by every word of God.*

Revelation 1:3 — *Blessed is he that readeth, and they that hear the words of this prophecy, and keep those things which are written therein: for the time is at hand.*

For a Christian to NOT read his/her Bible, it is as foolish as a starving man trapped in a huge supermarket on FREE-FOOD-DAY, ... yet he still refuses to eat and piecemeal dies of starvation! Jesus said in Matthew/Luke 4:4 that we need the Word of God as our spiritual food for a steady spiritual growth. Christians who don't read their Bibles epitomize the term: "walking contradiction" and literally MAKE NO SENSE!!!

God wants us to be balanced. (Proverbs 11:1.)

We will have no spiritual homeostasis if we don't read our Bibles; instead we will become categorically barren within and spiritually impoverished—not even realizing it, utterly desensitized by fleshly, worldly meaningless nonsense.

We, Christians who don't read our Bibles, in keeping with what ensues in our character from not reading the Bible constitute an end-over-end embarrassment to Christendom.

Proverbs 1:7 — *The fear of the LORD is the beginning of knowledge: but fools despise wisdom and instruction.*

People who don't read the Bible likewise despise wisdom and instruction.

Proverbs 1:22, says that fools hate knowledge. (Read it for yourself.)

Psalm 92:6 — *A brutish man knoweth not; neither doth a fool understand this.*

Lack of Bible reading renders us brutish!

This was not written to those who want to read the Bible but just don't understand it, yet still attend church, this was written to those who are starving for God's word, don't realize it, and yet persist in spiritual starvation without implementing the remedy. I'm not trying to insult, affront or malign one's character to those who don't read God's word. I'm trying to scream out to everyone, myself included, that if you are not reading your Bible, you are SPIRITUALLY STARVING, rotting from within. The only message I'm trying to convey in this subset is ... READ YOUR BIBLE!

If you, the reader still won't read your Bible after reading this then you have major issues with: me, God, Jesus, the Holy Spirit, the word, and yourself!

I'm spiritually starving right now for not reading my Bible ... so I will make this short. Satan wants us to stop reading our Bibles and then excuse such negligence! We may ignorantly think that not reading the Bible is no big deal, but it is! We become jerks and losers when we stop reading it. We are profane even in our thoughts if we neglect Bible-reading. If you disagree, it proves that you are resting cozily in some self-affirmed form of human moralism. That makes God sick. Isaiah 64:6.

You will never hear me say: *do this, do that, repent, be good, give up your sins, be a better person.* No. For those things aren't even possible if we don't read God's word daily and pray!

But I will never relent in telling people especially myself to … read your Bible!

Many will be angered at me for writing this and they will think that I'm just pontifically telling them what to do with harsh diatribe. But if they think that, they have failed to receive the point of my message. So, I will reiterate in triplicate!

READ YOUR BIBLE!

READ YOUR BIBLE!

READ YOUR BIBLE!!!!!!!!!!

Here's a good place to start.

Romans 12:1-21.

Basic **I**nstructions **B**efore **L**eaving **E**arth. A good place to start when it comes to how a person should live is found in the book of Romans. Romans 12, the whole chapter.

1—I beseech you therefore, brethren, by the mercies of God, that ye present your bodies a living sacrifice, holy, acceptable unto God, which is your reasonable service.

In verse 1 Paul is beseeching us to present our bodies as living sacrifices. That just means to deny ourselves worldly things. He does not demand this because that would be "works." We are saved by grace not works, (Romans 11:6) so Paul beseeches us to abstain from worldliness.

2—And be not conformed to this world: but be ye transformed by the renewing of your mind, that ye may prove what is that good, and acceptable, and perfect, will of God.

Be not conformed to the things of this world. Like politics, worldly movies, television, sports, drugs, the media, and other meaningless junk. Colossians 3:1-3 and 2 Corinthians 4:18 encourage us to focus on heaven as opposed to the worthless crud of this world!

3—For I say, through the grace given unto me, to every man that is among you, not to think of himself more highly than he ought to think; but to think soberly, according as God hath dealt to every man the measure of faith.

Use your gifts wisely and don't get conceited like the hypocritical Pharisees!

4—For as we have many members in one body, and all members have not the same office.

5—So we, being many, are one body in Christ, and every one members one of another.

6—Having then gifts differing according to the grace that is given to us, whether prophecy, let us prophesy according to the proportion of faith.

4,5,6 speak of our spiritual gifts and it also shows us that we as Christians are all part of one unitive body and are to function as one in unison.

7—Or ministry, let us wait on our ministering: or he that teacheth, on teaching.

Be patient. Good teaching may take some time.

8—Or he that exhorteth, on exhortation: he that giveth, let him do it with simplicity; he that ruleth, with diligence; he that sheweth mercy, with cheerfulness.

We should give cheerfully and exhort one another with simplicity. We should govern authoritatively yet diplomatically.

9—Let love be without dissimulation. Abhor that which is evil; cleave to that which is good.

Let our love be without bias. James 2:9 says that if we are a respecter of persons we commit sin. We are also to latch onto that which is good, not evil.

10—Be kindly affectioned one to another with brotherly love; in honour preferring one another.

We are to be kind to one another and to put others before ourselves. Others are much more interesting than we are.

11—Not slothful in business; fervent in spirit; serving the Lord.

We should not be lazy; lazing around watching television is a heinous sin. And we should cheerfully serve one another in any capacity that we have.

12—Rejoicing in hope; patient in tribulation; continuing instant in prayer.

We should praise God as it says in Psalms 34. And we should pray without ceasing as it says in 1 Thessalonians 5:17.

13—Distributing to the necessity of saints; given to hospitality.

We should be hospitable to our fellow Christians.

14—Bless them which persecute you: bless, and curse not.

Love your enemies. Even bless them. Don't cuss!

15—Rejoice with them that do rejoice, and weep with them that weep.

Don't be afraid to cry for those who hurt.

16—Be of the same mind one toward another. Mind not high things, but condescend to men of low estate. Be not wise in your own conceits.

Don't be arrogant and stay doctrinally likeminded. We should not have divisions in the church over doctrinal issues. Many will say that we should uphold certain doctrines and that is true, but we should never just agree to disagree over an important issue and then walk away with a disparity of opinions; that too is fostering a division.

17—Recompense to no man evil for evil. Provide things honest in the sight of all men.

Don't be vengeful when someone wrongs you!

18—If it be possible, as much as lieth in you, live peaceably with all men.

Live in peace, diplomacy, and not in loud, contentious chaos like unbelievers!

19—Dearly beloved, avenge not yourselves, but rather give place unto wrath: for it is written, Vengeance is mine; I will repay, saith the Lord.

God will repay those who wrong you.

20—Therefore if thine enemy hunger, feed him; if he thirst, give him drink: for in so doing thou shalt heap coals of fire on his head.

Be kind to your enemies, even pray for them.

21—Be not overcome of evil, but overcome evil with good.

Stay away from that which we know is evil. Vampires, magic, hatred, lust, filth, profanity, depravity, decadence, materialism, dark occultic things, false doctrine, witchcraft, sensuality, greed, secularity! Romans 12:1-21 is a template for basic instructional Christian living.

 Faith Alone. THE WAY TO GOD.

Chapter 19

Making A Gospel Tract

Many gospel tracts I find in bathroom stalls or on the aisle of a public bus are well intended but don't line up with scripture when explaining how a person is saved from the fires of hell. The Bible makes it simple. *Believe on the Lord Jesus Christ. By grace are ye saved through faith. I am the door. Whosoever will. Drink the gift of eternal life freely.* Such scriptural snippets are all legitimate if proper explanation is harmonized.

But many of the gospel tracts I've read, including the famous Chick tracts aren't so simple and accurate. They add the misrepresented step of repentance or a verbal confession and sometimes even the sinners prayer. The Bible never adds such requirements. A person is saved by simply believing in Jesus for eternal life. (1 Timothy 1:16.)

The best gospel tract is one that aligns with the scripture. Short, sweet and to the point. It needs ample biblical information but never too much. The ideal paradigm should look like this:

God loves you!

He sent his son, Jesus Christ to die for all of your sins.

All you have to do is believe in Jesus and you will live forever in heaven.

John 20:31 — *But these are written that you may believe that Jesus is the Christ, the son of God, and that believing you may have (everlasting) life in His name.*

It isn't wrong to put 'everlasting' in parenthesis because that is the context of John 20:31. Eternal life in Christ Jesus. Gospel tracts need to be in brevity because some or even most people don't like to read. If you give them what appears to be a novelette that turns them off. Make the gospel tract appealing and with much love. Refrain from the words: 'repent' or 'repentance.' Paul and Silas never said anything about repenting when they gave the gospel to the Philippian jailer.

Acts 16:29-31.

Then he called for a light, and sprang in, and came trembling, and fell down before Paul and Silas, And brought them out, and said, Sirs, what must I do to be saved? And they said, Believe on the Lord Jesus Christ, and thou shalt be saved, and thy house.

No mention of the word repent.

Just simple gospel.

Believe on the Lord Jesus Christ and you shall be saved.

Here is probably the best illustration of the believing the gospel.

Romans 10:10 — *For with the heart man believeth unto righteousness; and with the mouth confession is made unto salvation.*

Salvation, or imputed righteousness is by believing and believing is a heart issue. So many people based on flaws in their theology have added some type of emotionalism to their so-called "faith experience." They feel that real faith must be objectified by some type of ritual or change of behavior when the Bible is pervasively silent on this subject. Faith is simply being convinced that something is true. Read the subset entitled: <u>mental assent</u> for more on this subject.

I made a gospel tract out of a business card. I used a cloudy blue and white backdrop and then the gospel message in white letters. It reads easily! But sad to say it could read even easier. Another gospel tract could read for example.

God loves you and sent His son to die for you.

If you believe in Jesus you will go to heaven.

If you don't believe in Jesus you will go to hell.

John 3:36 — *He that believeth on the Son (Jesus) hath everlasting life: and he that believeth not the Son (Jesus) shall not see life; but the wrath of God abideth on him.*

This may be a bit frightening but it works. Children will understand this and get saved. John 6:45. Because of all the phony gospel tracts floating about, we should make our own gospel tracts according to the free grace message of the Bible. Here is a hypothetical example of how NOT to make a gospel tract:

You are a dirty, rotten sinner and are going straight to hell.

God does love you but you must repent of your sins and promise to follow God for the rest of your lives! Go and sin no more.

That's not the gospel!

In fact, that is Satan's gospel.

The real gospel is, 'believe on the Lord Jesus for eternal life.'

Let's make our self-made gospel tracts a true reflection of the Bible's message to mankind. John 3:16.

Here's another good example of a gospel tract.

God loves you and wants you to go to heaven forever.

Jesus died for all your sins so that you can have eternal life. Do you believe this?

My favorite method is to just make the gospel succinct. Six words. ((((**Believe in Jesus for eternal life.**))) Everything is laid out plainly and sweetly.

I could write a whole novel on the fact that we are all sinners on our way to hell. Christ died for your sins (1 Corinthians 15:3-4) so that we can be with Him in paradise forever. All we <u>must</u> do and <u>can</u> do is believe on Him for eternal life. Believing means to personally trust in Him for salvation. Once we believe in Him for eternal life, we are eternally secure. Once saved always saved! And this is all wonderfully true! But in six simple words, I can most aptly convey the entire gospel. "**Believe in Jesus for eternal life!**" The exciting thing about making your own gospel tract is that you can be as free and creative as you want to be. (1 Corinthians 9:18.) The key however is to stick with simple scriptures like:

Galatians 3:26 — *For ye are all the children of God by faith in Christ Jesus.*

The three essentials to gospel-tract contextualizing are:

1. Jesus.

2. Believing.

3. Everlasting life.

The next subset, I hope and pray, will assist you in gospel contextualization.

Faith alone. THE WAY TO CHRIST.

Chapter 20

Contextualizing the Gospel

Gospel contextualization is very important because some people worship God unbiblically. In Acts 17 the pagan Athenians were worshipping God under the rubric of: the unknown God.

For as I passed by, and beheld your devotions, I found an altar with this inscription, TO THE UNKNOWN GOD. Whom therefore ye ignorantly worship, him declare I unto you.

They needed a teacher or preacher to spell it out for them. This is gospel contextualization. Cornelius was worshipping God before the simple gospel message had been to him clearly contextualized.

Acts 10:30-31 — *And Cornelius said, Four days ago I was fasting until this hour; and at the ninth hour I prayed in my house, and, behold, a man stood before me in bright clothing, And said, Cornelius, thy prayer is heard, and thine alms are had in remembrance in the sight of God.*

But if you keep on reading in Acts 10, the gospel is clearly given. Whether Cornelius was saved before hearing the clear gospel or after is irrelevant, howbeit I think he was beforehand. The fact of the matter is that people need to know the clear Sola Fide gospel so that they can exponentially promulgate it to others. Here is when the gospel was received and contextualized.

Acts 10:43 — *To him give all the prophets witness, that through his name whosoever believeth in him shall receive remission of sins.*

Key words: "whosoever believed." What resulted in them believing in Christ? Remission of sins. Salvation. Everlasting life!

Below is an example of how you could contextualize the gospel.

1. Jesus died for your sins. All you have to do is believe in Him and you will go to heaven. 2. Man cannot save himself. Trying is useless. But Jesus Christ who died for all your sins, past, present, and future offers eternal life freely to anyone who will have it. His blood is enough to satisfy the wrath of God. All you have to do is come to him at one moment in time and place faith in him and you will undoubtedly be saved.

2. Salvation is a free gift and all you have to do is receive it by believing. Salvation cannot be lost and you can't give it back.

3. Once you are saved by relinquishing all trust in saving yourself by not sinning and doing good deeds you will have peace with God. You are justified by faith alone in Christ alone. He is the object of your faith like the Ark was in the days of Noah and the Noahic flood.

4. Just as the serpent was raised up by Moses in the wilderness so must the son of God be erected high so that anyone who believes in Jesus will have eternal life in heaven. Salvation is free. Salvation by faith alone in Jesus Christ is eternally secure.

5. False teachers are those who try to put one another back under some undoable law. They are condemned of themselves. 6. We are saved by abundant grace, grace upon

grace and the more we sin the more grace pours out upon us.

7. God loves sinners and is patient and merciful to anyone who calls upon His name. Jesus came to save that which is lost.

8. God loves everybody and is not a respecter of person. He desires to have everyone saved by faith alone in Christ alone. This guarantees eternal life.

9. Jesus Christ is the Son of God and Guarantor of eternal life simple to those who put faith in Him. 10. God demonstrated his love to all sinners so that they may have life, peace, joy and wisdom simply by believing in Christ.

What's the point of this? The point is that when giving the gospel to people sometimes the scripture needs to be contextualized. It is not adding to scripture or changing scripture so you don't have to worry about Proverbs 30:6 rendering you a liar. You are simply contextualizing.

Here's an example.

1 John 5:1 — *Whosoever believeth that Jesus is the Christ is born of God: and every one that loveth him that begat loveth him also that is begotten of him.*

Someone may not know what "Jesus is the Christ" means.

You don't have to change the text but you should explain that Jesus is the Guarantor of eternal life and that being born of God means you have it right here and now.

Another example would be:

Proverbs 8:35 — *For whoso findeth me findeth life, and shall obtain favour of the LORD.*

Because of this verse's prophetic nature you might want to put in parenthesis. Whoso findeth me (Jesus Christ) findeth life and shall obtain favour of the Lord. This is not adding to scripture; it is simply contextualizing the scripture. Someone may not know that Proverbs 8 is prophetic and may think that this verse was talking about King Solomon offering life. That would be taking the verse ridiculously out of context.

Contextualizing the gospel is extremely important when explaining the saving message to children. And it is incumbent upon proactive soul-winners to make the gospel as simple and understandable as possible.

Faith alone in Christ alone.

Chapter 21

The Kingdom of God Versus The Kingdom of Heaven

Salvation is simply by faith alone in Christ alone.

Galatians 5:5 — *For we through the Spirit wait for the hope of righteousness by faith.*

But some scriptures seem to allude to the idea that works are necessary for salvation as well.

Let me explain.

There's a lot of confusion between the Kingdom of heaven versus the Kingdom of God.

The Kingdom of God is an entrance into heaven.

The Kingdom of heaven denotes rewards or inheritance in heaven and in some cases it is referring to the millennial kingdom.

Luke 18:24 — *And when Jesus saw that he was very sorrowful, he said, How hardly shall they that have riches <u>enter</u> into the kingdom of God!*

Entering the Kingdom of God is contingent upon belief or faith only. The riches and the refusal to let them go were deterring this faith.

Notice that where the <u>Kingdom of Heaven</u> is mentioned in scripture it is always contingent upon some kind of works.

Matthew 3:2 — *And saying, <u>Repent</u> ye: for the kingdom of heaven is at hand.*

Repentance is a work. Changing your mind, turning from sin. Jonah 3:10.

Sometimes repentance accompanies faith, sometimes it precedes faith and sometimes it comes after faith, but come what may, it is not what saves a person.

Matthew 4:17 — *From that time Jesus began to preach, and to say, Repent: for the kingdom of heaven is at hand.*

Matthew 5:19 — *Whosoever therefore shall break one of these least commandments, and shall teach men so, he shall be called the least in the kingdom of heaven: but whosoever shall do and teach them, the same shall be called great in the kingdom of heaven.*

This has to be referring to rewards in heaven because it is predicated on: "doing," "teaching," "not breaking the commandments." All such actions are works.

Romans 4:5 — *But to him that worketh <u>not</u>, but believeth on him that justifieth the ungodly, his faith is counted for righteousness.*

Take a look at some other verses that are specifically referring to rewards in heaven; not entrance.

Matthew 5:20 — *For I say unto you, That except your righteousness shall exceed the righteousness of the scribes and Pharisees, ye shall in no case enter into the kingdom of heaven.*

Here is a Lewis Sperry Chafer, paraphrased quote.

Exposition of this passage is unnecessary. It is the foundation of all the demands for entrance into the kingdom of heaven, (rewards). It should in no wise be confused with entrance into heaven through the finished work of Christ Jesus. (Titus 3:5.) Unquote.

Matthew 13:24 — *Another parable put he forth unto them, saying, The kingdom of heaven is likened unto a man which sowed good seed in his field.*

Once again, this is referring to rewards. Sowing a good seed is a work. It is clear that salvation is a gift. You can't work for a gift!

Romans 6:23 — *For the wages of sin is death, but the gift of God is eternal life through Jesus Christ our Lord.*

Now, let's analyze the meaning of kingdom of God.

John 3:3 — *Jesus answered and said unto him, Verily, verily, I say unto thee, Except a man be born again, he cannot see the kingdom of God.*

What is the qualification of seeing or entering the kingdom of God?

Being born again.

How are we born again?

Belief in Christ!

Galatians 2:16 — *Knowing that a man is not justified by the works of the law, but by the faith of Jesus Christ, even we have believed in Jesus Christ, that we might be justified by the <u>faith of Christ</u>, and not by the works of the law: for by the works of the law shall no flesh be justified.*

The belief (our part) is what saves us.
Jesus' faith (His part) is what keeps us saved.

Look at this verse again.

"Justified by the faith of Christ."

It is not only our faith but Christ's faith that justifies us and we both know that Jesus isn't going to change His faith.

Malachi 3:6 — *For I am the LORD, <u>I change not</u>; therefore ye sons of Jacob are not consumed.*

We are promised entrance into heaven simply by believing.

Galatians 3:22 — *But the scripture hath concluded all under sin, that the promise by faith of Jesus Christ might be given to them that believe.*

Matthew 7:13 — *Enter ye in at the strait gate: for wide is the gate, and broad is the way, that leadeth to destruction, and many there be which go in thereat.*

What is this verse talking about?

It is talking about what one must do to be saved. Let me make you a grocery list of things to do in order to be saved and you tell me if it seems as if I'm giving wide qualifications for destruction.

Works.

Baptism.

Confession.

Speaking in tongues.

Legalism.

Fasting.

Animal sacrifices.

Circumcision.

Abstention from sin.

Church attendance.

Prayer.

If these things had to be done in order to be saved, the path wouldn't be narrow. The narrowness denotes that the only thing one has to do in order to be saved is to believe on Christ Jesus. Straight, narrow, simple, perfect and to the point. But some people say that you have to repent before believing and they use this verse to proof-text their case.

Mark 1:15 — *And saying, The time is fulfilled, and the kingdom of God is at hand: repent ye, and believe the gospel.*

Repentance precedes belief here. Yeah, but let's take a closer look at this. These people weren't believers. We both know that belief is the only requirement for salvation. John 3:16. John 3:36. John 5:24. John 6:47. Luke 7:50.

Acts 10:43. Acts 16:31.

Repentance (change of mind) comes before belief in Mark 1:15 because the people were in a state of unbelief otherwise it wouldn't say, "and believe the gospel." Belief is what saved them; repentance in this case is what enabled their belief. Here is a case in Acts where repentance followed belief.

Acts 11:21 — *And the hand of the Lord was with them: and a great number <u>believed</u>, and turned unto the Lord.*

The great number believed and then subsequently turned (repented) unto the Lord.

It may seem as if the initial repentance that leads to belief is a work. But belief itself is not the work. If a person wants to believe he is freely capable of believing. But for some people belief must be preceded by repentance—which is in this case exclusively turning away from unbelief. I.e., witchcraft, the occult, atheism, Islam, Buddhism, agnosticism, apathy.

All such practical worldviews are an expression of unbelief towards Christ.

So clearly, the difference between the Kingdom of God and the Kingdom of heaven are rewards and salvation.

Faith Alone. THE WAY TO CHRIST.

Chapter 22

Backsliding

Opponents of free grace will often condemn backsliders. Some Calvinists claim that backsliders prove to be fake Christians by the fact that they backslid or fell away from the Lord. They may use 1 John 2:19 to backup their claim, but this is too cut-and-dry— for nobody can know if a churchgoer has left the church to attend another church or if he has left because he is done with religion (Christianity). There is too much speculation in the Calvinism stance.

Arminians however claim that backsliders lose their salvation. Both suppositions are false. In fact, backsliding is a common thing in Christendom ... sad to say. What does the Bible say about backsliding?

Proverbs 14:14 — *The backslider in heart shall be filled with his own ways: and a good man shall be satisfied from himself.*

This verse proves that backsliders do exist.

In Hebrew the word for backslider is: *Cuwg*. Literally, it means someone who has retreated back to a previous way of conduct. A recidivist. To recidivate means to regress back to an olden or previous way of life. Like a reformed criminal going back to his criminalistic ways after rehabilitation.

Backsliding is something only a true believer can do. For a non-Christian to revert back to a non-Christian state makes no sense for non-Christians have always been in that state. So the term must apply only to believers. The question is ... what happens to backsliders. Arminians say they lose their salvation. Calvinists say they prove they never had it. But what does free grace theology say or better yet what does the Bible say?

Hosea 14:4 — *I will heal their backsliding, I will love them freely: for mine anger is turned away from him.*

Backsliders are forgiven and are still saved.

Are there any accounts in the Bible where true Christians backslid? The answer is: yes.

Jeremiah 3:6-8 — *The LORD said also unto me in the days of Josiah the king, Hast thou seen that which backsliding Israel hath done? she is gone up upon every high mountain and under every green tree, and there hath played the harlot. And I said after she had done all these things, Turn thou unto me. But she returned not. And her treacherous sister Judah saw it.*

Israel as a whole was in a backslidden state.

Verse 14 is the Lord exhorting them to turn from their back-slidden condition.

Turn, O backsliding children, saith the LORD; for I am married unto you: and I will take you one of a city, and two of a family, and I will bring you to Zion.

The fact that God says that He is married to Israel indicates that they are secure in Him positionally, but nevertheless He wishes for them to repent.

A backslidden Christian is common nowadays. But are they lost or will they be if they don't repent? The answer is no.

Jude 1:24, describes all believers and the security they can have in Christ.

Now unto him that is able to keep you from falling, and to present you faultless before the presence of his glory with exceeding joy.

Some skeptics of free grace may say that this is talking about apostasy. They may claim that God keeps all Christians from apostatizing and that if someone does apostatize that they were never really saved.

Well, then what did they apostatize from, an unsaved state to another unsaved state. Ridiculous! The word "falling" in this verse in the Greek is different than some other usages.

For instance.

2 Thessalonians 2:3 — *Let no man deceive you by any means: for that day shall not come, except there come a falling away first, and that man of sin be revealed, the son of perdition.*

Falling in this sense in Greek is *Apostasia*, which is where we get the anglicized: apostasy.

The Greek word in Jude 1:24 has a slightly different connotative nuance is: *Aptaistos*, which means standing firm positionally. When the scripture says:

<u>Now unto him that is able to keep you from falling</u>. It could be rendered.

<u>Now unto him that is able to keep you standing firm positionally</u>. Not necessarily experientially. This is God's promise even to the backslider.

Jude 1:24 further backs this up when it says:

And to present you faultless before the presence of his glory with exceeding joy.

God will present you faultless, not give you the ability to become faultless on our own which no Christian has the ability to do. So, even the backslider will be presented faultless. My encouragement is to repent and come back into a good stead of fellowship with God.

Matthew 3:2 — *And saying, Repent ye: for the kingdom of heaven is at hand.*

This could be used as an exhortation to the backslidden Christians everywhere. What causes someone to backslide?

It could be a number of things. A bad church experience, a vicissitude in one's vocation. A change of heart or a hardening of heart due to existential tragedy. It could be sin, worldly pleasure, or even just a change of environmental climate. Some people get on fire for God seasonally but then the fire overtime burns out. It could be Satan enticing them away from their spiritual walk, like in the parable of the sower and the soils. Luke 8:5-18.

Who knows?

I don't think that it happens overnight very often. It usually takes a graduation of events to cause spiritual declension.

We reach an upward gradient, and then due to circumstances, it plummets to a downward gradient low-point (nadir). This causes spiritual stagnancy, which over a long-term course of time evolves into a backslidden state.

So how do we prevent this?

There are many ways:

Stay in the word, in prayer, in church and in truth.

Faith Alone. THE WAY TO CHRIST!

Chapter 23

The Pharisees, The Prodigal Son, and Carnal Christians

Matthew 9:11 — *And when the Pharisees saw it, they said unto his disciples, Why eateth your Master with publicans and sinners?*

****

Luke 15:13 , v 32 — *And not many days after the younger son gathered all together, and took his journey into a far country, and there wasted his substance with riotous living.*

It was meet that we should make merry, and be glad: for this thy brother was dead, and is alive again; and was lost, and is found.

****

1 Corinthians 3:1 — *And I, brethren, could not speak unto you as unto spiritual, but as unto carnal, even as unto babes in Christ.*

There is no doubt that the unsaved can be and most of the time is: pharisaical, prodigal and carnal. But how unpopular is it to claim that the saved can be all three of these even for an extended period of time? The Pharisees, arrogant and supercilious, had a problem with sinners, the prodigal son had a problem with temperance, authority and spiritual living and the carnal Christian just preferred milk to meat.

So many people in the free grace camp will agree that even true Christians can and do become like them even seasonally. But what if we looked at this differently? What if we stopped viewing this with long-term lenses? Sure a person can be self-righteous and become pharisaical for a long period of time. Sure, a person can backslide and become prodigal for long interludes and likewise retain a carnal conduct.

But as Christians, we sin so frequently that I feel it is fair to say that we can become like anyone of these everyday, several times over. When we pray a harsh and judgmental prayer about our fellow sinner, we have become the Pharisee—even if it's only for ten minutes. When we get lazy, plop ourselves down in front of the tube with a bag of potato chips to watch secular television, we've become the prodigal son and remain that way until we turn the TV off and decide to pray or read our Bible.

When we neglect to witness to somebody for three straight days, we've become carnal. What people don't realize is that the characters in the Bible, prodigal, pharisaical, and carnal don't just represent people of longstanding behavior; they represent us everyday.

We may become the Pharisee 6 times a day. We may leave home and then return like the prodigal son 3 or 4 times a day. We may decide to stop reading our Bibles for a few consecutive days and be just as carnal as the church of Corinth.

The point is this…

We need to see ourselves in reflection of what scripture says. So many people only see the prodigals as those that have literally left home or the church long-term to live immoral, sloppy, sensuous and carnal lives when the truth is that every Christian becomes the prodigal son everyday even if it's only a few times for a few minutes!

When we look down on someone who wears an Austin 3:16 shirt, touts their homosexuality or cusses someone out we critically judge them. At such a time, we have become a hypocritical Pharisee! When we prefer watching a secular movie to a Bible study, we become carnal!

If we could see sin in a BIGGER light, we'd understand that the above-verses apply to all of us, not just a rare select few who make huge gaffes in their Christian walk.

Faith alone. THE WAY TO CHRIST.

Chapter 24

Law Versus Grace

This portion of Pauline scripture is a similitude of "law versus grace."

Romans 7:3-6.

3. *So then if, while her husband liveth, she be married to another man, she shall be called an adulteress: but if her husband be dead, she is free from that law; so that she is no adulteress, though she be married to another man.*

This is not a literal account of a married woman dealing with the issue of adultery. This is metaphor. The woman represents sinners. The marriage represents being under the law. The marriage to another man represents sin. If she sins while being under the law she is guilty—hence the term 'adulteress' is befitting. When it says, "if her husband be dead she is free from the law" this is referring to the freedom Christians have when Christ rendered us dead to the law by grace.

4. *Wherefore, my brethren, ye also are become dead to the law by the body of Christ; that ye should be married to another, even to him who is raised from the dead, that we should bring forth fruit unto God.*

This simply means that when we are saved, we are dead to the law, married to Christ and now able to bare fruit. When did we die to the law?

Galatians 2:20, tells us.

We died to the law when Christ died.

Galatians 2:20 — *I am crucified with Christ: nevertheless I live; yet not I, but Christ liveth in me: and the life which I now live in the flesh I live by the faith of the Son of God, who loved me, and gave himself for me.*

Before we were in Christ we were subject to the law an unable to bring forth fruits of life. While under the law, the only fruits (obedience) that we could bring forth were dead, worthless fruits.

So for those who deny free grace, they are still under the law and their righteousness is as scripture says, filthy rags. (Isaiah 64:6.)

Only in grace can we produce any real, worthwhile fruit.

5. *For when we were in the flesh, the motions of sins, which were by the law, did work in our members to bring forth fruit unto death.*

Once again, while under the law, the only thing we can produce is dead fruit.

6. *But now we are delivered from the law, that being dead wherein we were held; that we should serve in newness of spirit, and not in the oldness of the letter.*

When we are in Christ, we are saved by grace, no longer under the law, and free to serve God with no obligation. Free grace theology must emphasize this blessed truth.

I don't know about you, but I'd much rather serve in the newness of the spirit, which is what the free grace position espouses, than to serve in the oldness of the letter, which is what the anti-free-gracers are doing!

Q: Who is under the law?

A: Anyone that is not saved.

Galatians 5:18 — *But if ye be led of the Spirit, ye are not under the law.*

Q: Who is led by the spirit?

A: Christians.

So those who are lost are not led by the spirit, hence still under the law.

Q: Who else is under the law?

A: The anti-free-gracers.

They refuse to accept grace, so they are still under their own law.

Romans 2:14 — *For when the Gentiles, which have not the law, do by nature the things contained in the law, these, having not the law, are a law unto themselves.*

It is foolish to deny free grace because it puts you under the law, even when the law was abolished by grace.

Ephesians 2:15 — *Having abolished in his flesh the enmity, even the law of commandments contained in ordinances; for to make in himself of twain one new man, so making peace.*

Christians, who have accepted free grace, are not under the law. We have a new law. A law of love. A law that doesn't demand any obedience whatsoever but expects willful obedience out of love and gratitude.

Q: What is this law?

A: A simple commandment.

1 John 3:23 — *And this is his commandment, That we should believe on the name of his Son Jesus Christ, and love one another, as he gave us commandment.*

Some may be thinking, but isn't this putting us back under the law? Isn't the demand to believe and love one another a lawful demand. The answer is, no. Believing in Christ is not a meritorious act because it takes no effort—even for the hardhearted atheists that can't find it in themselves to believe in God. For him, it is not a matter of having a difficulty believing for he simply doesn't want to believe.

Now, the part about loving one another is not dutiful because forced, peremptory, mandatory or coerced love wouldn't be real love in the first place. Our love for one another flows from God's love in us. This doesn't mean that we will love people with a perfect Christlike love 24/7. Because only God can do that. This new commandment isn't even mandatory. When a person is under the law, they have to obey every law according to their own, warped system. (Galatians 3:10.)

But when in grace we are given a commandment that is to love one another. To say that if a person doesn't love one another, that he isn't in grace is to make grace into a work. Grace doesn't demand anything, but it does encourage. The keyword is "should," not "have to."

And this is his commandment, That we <u>should</u> believe on the name of his Son Jesus Christ, and (<u>should</u>) love one another, as he gave us commandment.

Emphasis mine.

Chafer makes a good law vs. grace dichotomy.

In place of the law there is grace.

In place of condemnation there is salvation.

In place of death there is life.

In place of ruin in Adam there is resurrection in Christ.

In place of bondage there is liberty.

In place of defeat there is victory.

In place of hell there is heaven.

Faith Alone. THE WAY TO CHRIST!

Chapter 25

Sin

Most people don't understand sin. They don't understand their own sin nature. They fail to see just how sinful they are according to scripture. The Bible makes it clear that the more we study the scripture and acquaint ourselves with the law, the more sinful we realize we are. Take a look at Romans 7:13.

Romans 7:23 — *Was then that which is good made death unto me? God forbid. But sin, that it might <u>appear</u> sin, working death in me by that which is good; that sin by the commandment might become exceeding sinful.*

I'm not saying that the law makes us more sinful, it does make our sinfulness appear more sinful. It's kind of like a telescope. It doesn't make the stars and planets bigger, but it does optically enlarge them from our standpoint. Imagine someone who has twenty-five bad habits. They are only aware of 6 of them. They read the Bible for three hours and are now aware of twelve of them. The Bible didn't give them six more habits, but it does make them aware of six new habits. The Bible doesn't make a person more sinful; it just makes us more aware of our sinfulness. Take a look at how easy it is to sin, according to the Bible.

1 Corinthians 15:34 — *Awake to righteousness, and sin not; for some have not the knowledge of God: I speak this to your shame.*

We can sin and not even have knowledge of it.

We can sin in ignorance.

Numbers 15:29 — *Ye shall have one law for him that sinneth through ignorance, both for him that is born among the children of Israel, and for the stranger that sojourneth among them.*

We have sins in our bones metaphorically speaking.

Job 20:11 — *His bones are full of the sin of his youth, which shall lie down with him in the dust.*

Psalm 51:1 — *Behold, I was shapen in iniquity; and in sin did my mother conceive me.*

We are born in sin, genetically. (John 3:6)

It is amiss to think that a Christian can tabulate his sins. For the Bible's criterion for what sin is and how vast are its entailments are astronomical. To think that we don't sin and sadly some Christians think this is foolish. The only thing that can result from thinking you don't sin it to err into pride, which is sin.

Proverbs 21:4 — *An high look, and a proud heart, and the plowing of the wicked, is sin.*

Foolishness is sin. That means that laughing at a dumb joke and engaging in idol chitchat renders you sinful.

Proverbs 24:9 — *The thought of foolishness is sin: and the scorner is an abomination to men.*

Jesus said that anyone who commits sin is a servant or slave to sin. This does not just include addicts or those caught up in habitual sins; this includes all sinners, believers and unbelievers.

John 8:34 — *Jesus answered them, Verily, verily, I say unto you, Whosoever committeth sin is the servant of sin.*

The Bible says that anything not of faith is sin. There are so many benighted Christians that don't think they are carnal. They plop themselves down on their recliner with their potato chips and soft drink and watch three hours of television. There is not a modicum of faith involved in this. This is sin! Pure, quintessential sin.

Romans 14:23 — *And he that doubteth is damned if he eat, because he eateth not of faith: for whatsoever is not of faith is sin.*

It doesn't stop here. Doing anything that is Christless is sin. Scripture says that to not abide in Christ is sin.

1 John 3:6 — *Whosoever abideth in him sinneth not: whosoever sinneth hath not seen him, neither known him.*

Going to the movies is not abiding in Christ unless it is a Christian movie. Idle chitchat about sports is not abiding in Christ. Any kind of activity where Christ is not incorporated in is not abiding in Christ and therefore sin!

Where does it end? Carnal Christians are those who fail to see their own filthy sinful status. Their wretched self-righteousness has them blind to how gross and putrid they really are. Stop thinking highly of yourselves and admit you are a sinner. Romans 12:3.

It is so easy to sin that the Bible says that if we have blood feuds with our neighbors we are sinning.

Proverbs 14:21 — *He that despiseth his neighbour sinneth: but he that hath mercy on the poor, happy is he.*

Imagine your crotchety, old neighbor throwing trash in your yard. This angers you; you get to where you literally despise him. That too is sin. Who's not guilty of this sin?

Committing sin is so easy that the Bible narrows it down to simply showing favoritism.

James 2:9 — *But if ye have respect to persons, ye commit sin, and are convinced of the law as transgressors.*

This doesn't mean that if we respect people we commit sin, this is talking about playing favorites. Respect to persons would be showing respect to one person but discriminating against others. Kind of like when grandma gives gifts to all her granddaughters but doesn't to her grandsons. That's being a respecter of persons. Sinning is so easy and prevalent that the Bible says that if we know to do good and don't do it that is sin.

James 4:17 — *Therefore to him that knoweth to do good, and doeth it not, to him it is sin.*

Your aunt sends you twenty dollars in the mail for your birthday and you get the whim to write her a "thank you" note, but don't do it. This is knowing to do what is good and not doing it. This is sin! Sin is serious business. Those who minimize it are affronting God's word on the issue.

1 John 5:17 — *All unrighteousness is sin: and there is a sin not unto death.*

It is the nature of man to deny his sin problem or to minimize it. This too is sin. This is denial.

Most people are deceived about how sinful they are and the Bible clarifies this.

Romans 7:11 — *For sin, taking occasion by the commandment, <u>deceived me</u>, and by it slew me.*

What is the point of addressing this issue? The more we know about sin the better we will be in defeating it. Those people who act as if they have overcome the power of sin are so deceived by sin that they just become an embarrassment to Christendom. They are like lepers who think that the only thing physically wrong with them is a few mosquito bites.

The point of this knowledge about sin is to point us to God's immeasurable grace.

When you minimize sin you minimize grace.

The only thing that ensues from self-righteousness is a hatred or indifference towards grace. It would be like me thinking that my monopoly money was legitimate capital.

With such a deluded notion I would shun real money under the deception that my funny money could buy me anything I wanted. That's the mentality of those who think that they can conquer sin on their own. They wax in disappointment when they find out that their funny money (self-confidence) was entirely worthless.

We need to never forget that salvation is a free gift and that:

Faith Alone is the way to Christ.

Chapter 26

Christian or Savedian

All believers in Christ are promised heaven. John 6:47. John 11:25-26. But does that mean that all Christians are sanctified? Does that mean that all Christians bear fruit? No. There are some Christians that shouldn't be called Christians. There's a distinction between a Christian and a disciple. The term disciple is not a permanent appellation for discipleship has an on/off switch. We are disciples when we are living in the spirit. We are not when we are living in sin. Disciples are made by special training. John 4:1. Those living in sin are not being trained to be disciples.

All Christians are carnal when they shut their Bibles and live after the flesh. You're carnal when you are in sin; you are spiritual when you are in the word, prayer, church, etc.

What about all this perseverance nonsense.

Calvinists use this verse to proof-text the doctrine of the perseverance of the saints.

Matthew 24:13 — *But he that shall endure unto the end, the same shall be saved.*

Saint Augustine misapplied this verse and made it the staple of his theology. He was an amillennialist who denied the fact that the tribulation and the millennial kingdom would succeed the rapture therefore according to his theology this verse must be referring to eternal salvation not tribulational salvation, which is merely temporal in nature. John Calvin at first purportedly held to the free grace position but in responding to the Catholic counter remonstrance, he took the Augustinian view of perseverance of the saints. Whether or not a person perseveres in the faith has nothing to do with their salvation. Matthew 24 in its entirety is about the tribulation. Those who endure to the end and don't accept the mark of the beast will be physically saved. This verse is referring to those left behind and has no application for today-Christians. It's horrible how two purportedly great theologians can, with one verse, mess up theology henceforth.

Christian living is an issue of sanctification. This is a lifelong process. But our sanctification is contingent upon us walking in the spirit, namely us reading the Bible.

John 17:17-19 — *Sanctify them through thy truth: thy word is truth. As thou hast sent me into the world, even so have I also sent them into the world. And for their sakes I sanctify myself, that they also might be sanctified through the truth.*

Our sanctification is contingent upon the reception of God's word. As teachers, and ministers we are to sanctify our followers by teaching them the word of God. We are to sanctify ourselves by reading the word of God on our own.

Many Christians don't read their Bible. This would qualify someone as a: Savedian.

Those who are just saved, I dub Savedians. They are believers who are in fact saved by grace but not living in the spirit. As Christians we must read our Bibles daily. If not our sanctification can be curbed even to the point of cessation. That's a good way to bring upon ourselves divine chastisement. (Hebrews 12:6-8, 10-11.)

The thief on the cross is a perfect example of a Savedian. He was indeed saved but not a disciple.

Luke 23:42-44 — *And he said unto Jesus, Lord, remember me when thou comest into thy kingdom. And Jesus said unto him, Verily I say unto thee, Today shalt thou be with me in paradise.*

Given no chance for discipleship, I would have to say that the thief on the cross was a Savedian. Saved he was. Jesus declared it. I just think that there are scads of Christians at large that should not bear the title Christian but should be dubbed Savedian. But this is not a permanent title. This is a fluctuant title. If you live like an unbeliever you're a Savedian during that season. When you live and or abide in Christ you are a Christian. This is just a matter of semantics. All believers are saved and Christians. I just think that in humility we should call ourselves Savedian at the times when we live after the flesh.

I'm not saying that we should go around to everyone that lazes around and doesn't read their Bible and call them a Savedian. This would not be Christlike for all of us even regenerate Christians sin.

A person dubbed Christian is one who reads their Bible, prays, goes to church, guards their tongue and exemplifies Christ in their daily character. A person who is dubbed Savedian is one who lives like the rest of the lost world, yet he is still saved.

Philippians 3:17-19 — *Brethren, be followers together of me, and mark them which walk so as ye have us for an ensample. (For many walk, of whom I have told you often, and now tell you even weeping, that they are the enemies of the cross of Christ: Whose end is destruction, whose God is their belly, and whose glory is in their shame, who mind earthly things.)*

Those who walk such a way are Savedians. For they are not acting like Christians. All believers in Christ are saved and on their way to heaven. 1 Thessalonians 5:10.

Savedian versus Christian is just a rhetorical distinction. Like babes in Christ versus disciple or carnal versus spiritual.

Faith Alone. THE WAY TO CHRIST.

Chapter 27

Fruit Inspection

In loving honor to Zane C Hodges; June 1932 - November 2008. His material helped me exegete this.

Who's ever heard this: *You'll know them by their fruits.* Here's how you know if you are saved. We start fruit inspecting. This is ludicrous. First of all, we can't determine whether or not we, ourselves or others are saved based on our fruits because 95 percent of all Christians are carnal or personified that way whilst not in church whereupon their facades are removed. Fruit inspection is dangerous. The Bible gives us real assurance of salvation based solely on the word of God.

We don't need to inspect our fruit because our shifty circumstances play a huge role in how we behave in our Christian walk. For instance, let's say that someone doubted their salvation while on the hectic highway during a storm of road-rage! That would not be a good time to inspect fruit. The Bible makes it clear that we can be sure that we are saved without fruit inspection.

1 Thessalonians 1:5 — *For our gospel came not unto you in word only, but also in power, and in the Holy Ghost, and in much assurance; as ye know what manner of men we were among you for your sake.*

God's word is powerful. (Hebrews 4:12.) The word, the power and Holy Ghost all assure us of salvation.

Here are a series of scriptures on so-called, "fruit inspection" that most people misinterpret.

Matthew 7:15-20.

15—Beware of false prophets, which come to you in sheep's clothing, but inwardly they are ravening wolves.

16—Ye shall know them by their fruits. Do men gather grapes of thorns, or figs of thistles?

17—Even so every good tree bringeth forth good fruit; but a corrupt tree bringeth forth evil fruit.

18—A good tree cannot bring forth evil fruit, neither can a corrupt tree bring forth good fruit.

19—Every tree that bringeth not forth good fruit is hewn down, and cast into the fire.

20—Wherefore by their fruits ye shall know them.

These verses have been misinterpreted as to refer to a person's works or deeds. His good deeds and bad deeds are his fruit, they say. Wrong! This can't be talking about works.

The false prophet is a wolf in sheep's clothing. His works and sins are being hidden otherwise he'd be a wolf in wolf's clothing, not a wolf in sheep's clothing. The fruits here are referring to his teaching or "words." He may seem saintly but his teachings are heretical. Let's be more logical about this. Think about it. If a person's "fruits" were his "good works" then how do we know if his motives were pure? A person may help an old lady cross the road only to mug and rob her whilst no one is looking. Surely, what looks like a good deed may in fact be crookedness. This fruit/works conjecture just doesn't work in determining if someone is saved!

Some may disagree with this and still maintain that the fruits are the works or deeds. Well if that were true then this would logically lead to sinless perfection.

Look at verse 18 again.

A good tree <u>cannot</u> bring forth evil fruit, neither can a corrupt tree bring forth good fruit.

If the "evil fruit" were referring to sins, then this is suggesting that a Christian no longer sins. This is unbiblical.

1 John 1:8, v10, Romans 3:23. Ecclesiastes 7:20. Romans 3:10-12. Jeremiah 3:22.

Clearly, fruits in these passages, are not talking about deeds.

Take a look at the comparative language in the following verses in the same gospel.

Matthew 12:33-37.

Either make the tree good, and his <u>fruit</u> good; or else make the tree corrupt, and his fruit corrupt: for the tree is known by his fruit.

34—O generation of vipers, how can ye, being evil, speak good things? for out of the abundance of the heart the mouth speaketh. (This denotes words or teachings)

35—A good man out of the good treasure of the heart bringeth forth good things: and an evil man out of the evil treasure bringeth forth evil things.

36—But I say unto you, That every idle word that men shall speak, they shall give account thereof in the day of judgment.

37—For by thy <u>words</u> thou shalt be justified, and by thy <u>words</u> thou shalt be condemned.

The fruits of either good teachers or false teachers are their words. Lordship Salvationists are false teachers and their heresies can be known as bad fruits, by the which they shall be judged.

Fruit inspection is not necessary in the free grace camp. God's word is all the assurance you need. 1 John 5:13. Romans 4:16. 1 Thessalonians 1:4-5. John 6:69.

Faith Alone is the way to Christ.

Chapter 28

Eternal Rewards

Revelation 20:12 — *And I saw the dead, small and great, stand before God; and the books were opened: and another book was opened, which is the book of life: and the dead were judged out of those things which were written in the books, according to their works.*

Most preachers don't put much emphasis on eternal rewards. Lordship Salvation proponents shouldn't put any emphasis on eternal rewards because in their theology it's all about making it to heaven so eternal rewards are not even in their train of thought. Salvation is a free gift (John 4:10, Romans 6:23). So therefore eternal rewards are costly. But we are here to earn rewards in heaven. That is our motivation for doing good works in this lifetime. One good way to start is to read the Bible. It promises blessings.

Luke 11:28 — *But he said, Yea rather, blessed are they that hear the word of God, and keep it.*

The Bible makes it clear that we will be judged according to our works whether they are good or bad.

2 Corinthians 5:10 — *For we must all appear before the judgment seat of Christ; that every one may receive the things done in his body, according to that he hath done, whether it be good or bad.*

Rewards are going to be characterized by six materials. Word, hay and stubble or gold silver or precious stones.

Take a look at:

1 Corinthians 3:11-15.

11—For other foundation can no man lay than that is laid, which is Jesus Christ.

12—Now if any man build upon this foundation gold, silver, precious stones, wood, hay, stubble;

13—Every man's work shall be made manifest: for the day shall declare it, because it shall be revealed by fire; and the fire shall try every man's work of what sort it is.

14—If any man's work abide which he hath built thereupon, he shall receive a reward.

15—If any man's work shall be burned, he shall suffer loss: but he himself shall be saved; yet so as by fire.

Obviously the good works, gold, silver and precious stones will withstand the fire and hence be eternal.

Ephesians 6:8 — *Knowing that whatsoever good thing any man doeth, the same shall he receive of the Lord, whether he be bond or free.*

This simply means that anyone can earn rewards is heaven for doing good deeds whilst here on earth.

Matthew 6:18-20 — *That thou appear not unto men to fast, but unto thy Father which is in secret: and thy Father, which seeth in secret shall reward thee openly.*

Lay not up for yourselves treasures upon earth, where moth and rust doth corrupt, and where thieves break through and steal: But lay up for yourselves treasures in heaven, where neither moth nor rust doth corrupt, and where thieves do not break through nor steal.

This is the very reason we should be focused on heaven, (Colossians 3:2). It will avail us heavenly rewards. Free grace theology is very emphatic on earning eternal rewards. Whose ever heard someone say that they don't care if they earn eternal rewards in heaven they'll just be happy to get there. That is a horrific way to be. That reveals just how carnal a person is. We should gladly desire to earn heavenly rewards. That's one of the reasons for doing good works, like: Bible reading, evangelizing, praying, church attendance, etc, etc. If you deviate from the free grace message of the Bible you lose the doctrine of eternal rewards entirely.

Isaiah 3:10 — *Say ye to the righteous, that it shall be well with him: for they shall eat the fruit of their doings.*

Galatians 6:7 — *Be not deceived; God is not mocked: for whatsoever a man soweth, that shall he also reap.*

Genesis 49:25 — *Even by the God of thy father, who shall help thee; and by the Almighty, who shall bless thee with blessings of heaven above, blessings of the deep that lieth under, blessings of the breasts, and of the womb.*

Proverbs 28:20 — *A faithful man shall abound with blessings: but he that maketh haste to be rich shall not be innocent.*

Ephesians 1:3 — *Blessed be the God and Father of our Lord Jesus Christ, who hath blessed us with all spiritual blessings in heavenly places in Christ.*

Revelation 22:12 — *And, behold, I come quickly; and my reward is with me, to give every man according as his work shall be.*

Faith Alone. THE WAY TO CHRIST.

Addendum

Faith alone is our way to Christ and Christ's way to us. It has to be this way. If Christ did all the work in freely giving us eternal life than the only requirement is simple, childlike faith that Jesus is the Guarantor of eternal life. He offered Himself to us 2000 years ago at Calvary. Salvation is about receiving Christ—Colossians 2:6—the only way to do so is by faith alone. Ephesians 3:8-9, John 1:12. Galatians 3:26.

I'm glad the Bible makes it clear that we must do things God's way. Proverbs 14:12.

Indubitably, God's way unto salvation is by faith alone in Christ alone. It has been said that faith is the courage to accept the acceptance of Christ. I wholeheartedly agree.

Matt.

JESUS

A
V
E
S

11099857R00094

Made in the USA
San Bernardino, CA
09 May 2014